D0147371

'As a specialist autism professional, an adopter and an ex-foster carer, I found this book is a joy to read! It is rare that a book by professionals is so accessible. Katie Hunt and Helen Rodwell have been able to use their knowledge and skills to great effect but taken into account the importance of reaching their audience of very busy people who will have a wide variation in academic skills.'

– *Heather Moran, Consultant Child Clinical Psychologist, Coventry and Warwickshire Partnership Trust, NHS UK, Author of* The Coventry Grid

An Introduction to
Autism for Adoptive and Foster Families

How to Understand and Help Your Child

KATIE HUNT AND HELEN RODWELL

Foreword by Daniel Hughes

Jessica Kingsley *Publishers*
London and Philadelphia

First published in 2019
by Jessica Kingsley Publishers
73 Collier Street
London N1 9BE, UK
and
400 Market Street, Suite 400
Philadelphia, PA 19106, USA

www.jkp.com

Library of Congress Cataloging in Publication Data
A CIP catalog record for this book is available from the Library of Congress

British Library Cataloguing in Publication Data
A CIP catalogue record for this book is available from the British Library

ISBN 978 1 78592 405 7
eISBN 978 1 78450 759 6

Printed and bound in the United States

Katie Hunt: Thanks to all the schools, autistic children and their families, and colleagues who I have worked with for teaching me so much.

Helen Rodwell: To my parents and all of the brilliant children and families I have worked with.

Contents

List of figures

Foreword

This is such an important and comprehensive book by Katie Hunt and Helen Rodwell! It is written with a conversational tone that is easy to read and understand, while still providing a great deal of important knowledge that is clearly presented. This would be an excellent resource for both foster and adoptive families and families with an autistic child. It is truly a superlative book for understanding and caring for a child with autism who also is adopted or in foster care.

This book covers too much to mention here, but it must be said that the core principles of care and related interventions, as well as the 'tricky situations' that need to be addressed, are covered in a sound and thorough manner. Along the way, the authors present an insightful description of the severe challenges and many diverse transitions that these children encounter – along with interventions that help them to face them. There is an excellent presentation of attachment, trauma and loss, something certainly considered in understanding and helping foster and adopted children, but too often overlooked in considering the special challenges in addressing these themes that are faced by children with autism. Hunt and Rodwell's work is more than an Introduction to Autism. It is a wonderful guide to understanding and helping these children, written in a manner that will be of great value to professionals, carers, and parents alike.

Daniel Hughes, Ph.D.
Founder of Dyadic Developmental
Psychotherapy and President of DDPI
South Portland, Maine, USA

Acknowledgments

Our aim in writing this book has been to talk about autism in a straightforward and accessible way so that busy parents can understand it and think about what it means for their child. We have used a conversational tone and tried to avoid jargon and detailed references. This runs the risk of us having over-simplified or misrepresented some complex ideas, but we hope that the usefulness of this book makes it okay. We have of course been influenced by many authors, researchers and clinicians. We want to acknowledge many people and we hope that we have represented your work adequately: John Bowlby, Mary Ainsworth, Dan Siegel, Heather Moran, Tony Attwood, Alis Rowe and Carol Gray.

Our understanding of all things autism-related is constantly developing through our work with parents and children and through discussion with our colleagues. We want to thank all of the children and parents who have shared their experiences with us. Thanks also to Dr Anna Moore Asgharian, Lee Rodwell and Jane Massey for your ideas and feedback on drafts – you've made this book better!

Preface

Being a parent to any child can be a mix of joy and challenges. Being a parent to a fostered or adopted child can add extra challenges because your child has usually had a difficult start to life. Your child has undoubtedly experienced some form of loss, trauma or neglect, which add many extra things for you to understand so that you can help her to recover and settle in your family. Adding autism into the mix can add further questions, concerns and complexities.

You are probably reading this book because you are parenting a child with autism or perhaps are about to. Or, you may be parenting a child who you, or others, suspect may have autism. We hope that this book provides you with accessible and practical information about autism to help you as a parent.

We have organised this book into two main parts. The first part tells you about autism – what it is and how it is diagnosed. We touch upon the different professionals who may be involved with your child. We look at what can be generally helpful when parenting your child. The second part focuses on some of the extra things that come along when your child is fostered or adopted. We explore placement transitions, contact, attachments and how to help your child with her life story and experiences of loss and trauma. We include a brief chapter on looking after yourself, which, although it comes late in the book, is an essential foundation for parenting.

We are mindful that when writing about autism it can be easy to make sweeping generalisations that would not fit all children. No two children are the same, and this is certainly the case for autism. Each child is unique. We are also mindful that many assumptions are made about children with autism, for example that their lives are full of problems and challenges. Children with autism, like all children, have many wonderful attributes and strengths. As you read this book, we want to encourage you to reflect upon your own child, her individuality, particular qualities and strengths, as well as her challenges. We particularly want to encourage you to use the information in this book to get to know your child and her autism. Take what is useful for your child rather than following any of the ideas too rigidly. You, as her parent, are usually the best person to know her and what she needs from you as a parent.

Notes on terminology

Throughout the book we use the word 'parent' to describe birth parents, kinship carers, foster carers and adoptive parents who provide an everyday parenting role for the child they are caring for.

We have alternated between male and female throughout the book in order to avoid clumsiness. We use the word 'child' and 'children' to include all children aged from 0 to 18.

We want to acknowledge that the ways people can interact, communicate and parent can vary within and between cultures. We are all influenced by our own culture, so we invite you to adapt the ideas to suit your child and your culture.

Chapter 1

What is Autism?

Introduction

In this chapter, we're going to give you an overview of autism, looking at some of the things that can be different for children with autism, how they see the world and some of the situations where there can be difficulties. We hope that by the end of this book, you'll have a good sense of what these might be and how to manage some of them.

All children are different, and what works for one child will not work for another; children with autism are no different in this respect. When we add being fostered or adopted into the mix then each child and their family becomes even more unique. This means that there are not always clear right and wrong answers about what to do, but we hope that you will go away from reading this book with some different ways of thinking about how to help your child.

> Every child with autism and their family is unique, so there are no right and wrong answers.

There are a few important points that we want to get across before we start.

- We want you to have a good understanding that autism is part of something that we call *social communication difficulties*.

- Children with autism do not necessarily have lots of *difficulties* – they may or may not have difficulties and very often the problems that autistic children have are created for them by things in the outside world.

- Not all children who could get a diagnosis of autism will actually have one. There are lots of reasons for this, and we'll talk about them in this and the next chapter.

- Some professionals will say that if a child does not have a diagnosis of autism then it means that they do not have social communication difficulties, but this is not true. We hope that anyone with a child who is struggling with social communication will find this book helpful.

You don't need your child to have a diagnosis of autism to find the issues and approaches in this book helpful. This book is for parents of a child with any kind of social communication difficulty.

What do we mean when we say 'autism'?

If you're reading this book then you've probably already heard of autism. We've already said that autism is a difficulty with social communication. Some (but not all) people think there may be a genetic component to it, although we don't have a good understanding of how any genetic element works. We do know that several people within a family might have autism, but we also know that in other families there is only one person who has autism.

Autism reflects difficulties with social communication.

Autism is a 'spectrum disorder'. We'll talk more about this later on, but it means that a child who has autism can have it to a greater or lesser degree. We've found that when people talk about the spectrum then it also invites the word 'disorder' to be used, but we don't feel that anyone with autism should have to be seen as 'disordered'.

Autism is a spectrum.

We're both Clinical Psychologists and we're keen to use language that correctly describes what we're talking about, but we know that it's not always easy for non-psychologists to get their heads round all the different terms and what they mean.

Professionals use a lot of different terms to describe children who meet formal criteria for autism. Research published in 2016, led by Lorcan Kenny,[1] found that people with autism and their carers also used lots of different terms. The terms people might use include:

- autism

- autism spectrum disorder (or ASD)

- on the autism spectrum

- Asperger's syndrome

- autistic features

- social communication difficulties

- pervasive developmental difficulties

- atypical autism

- high-functioning autism

- Pathological Demand Avoidance (or PDA).

---

1   You can find the reference for this and any other study we mention in Chapter 9.

There are probably even more terms than this. The point we want to make is that there are many terms around to describe people who struggle with social communication. We should be clear that, for lots of different reasons, we don't like all of these terms.

There is no one way of talking about children with autism that everyone agrees with. We are going to try to take a middle line, partly because we do not really understand what term children themselves would prefer. We will talk about 'autistic children' and 'children with autism' throughout this book, and we hope that we will not offend anyone by doing this. Whatever term you want to use is fine. These terms are shorthand ways of describing a set of differences, strengths and difficulties. You'll need to find the term that works best for you and your child.

> Children with autism do not *necessarily* have difficulties; being different from other people is not a difficulty.

As Clinical Psychologists, we tend to see children when they, or people around them, are having some kind of challenge with some aspect of behaviour. We know that not all of you reading this book will have sought help for 'problems' or 'difficulties', and we also know that not everyone with autism will see themselves as having difficulties, but we're going to be using the word 'difficulties' throughout this book.

We're going to try our best not to tie ourselves up in knots about the language we use (although you might think we have done that already). We might not always get it right. We want to apologise to anyone who feels that we are giving only a negative view of autism.

Phew! Now that we have dealt with what we are talking about, we can get on with talking about autism.

So, what is autism?

Autism is a lifelong set of differences with social communication that we think have a neurodevelopmental basis.

> Autism is considered to be a neurodevelopmental difficulty.

Neurodevelopmental difficulties can be hard to define. In essence:

- they are something a child is born with, although it might not be obvious until later on

- genetics, environment, family, pregnancy and things happening at, or around the time of, birth are all important in neurodevelopmental difficulties, along with other risk factors that might occur during a child's early development

- having a risk factor does not mean that difficulties are inevitable or that all children who share risk factors will have the same outcome, only that these things are *associated with* difficulties. Human behaviour and human development are hugely complex and there is so much that we don't fully understand.

Neurodevelopmental difficulties are not the same as learning disabilities, although some children with neurodevelopmental difficulties will also have a learning disability.

Confusingly, and just to add to the list of different terms that are in use, there are 'learning disabilities' and 'learning difficulties'.

- 'Learning disabilities' mean general difficulties with learning.

- 'Learning difficulties' mean specific problems with learning, such as dyslexia.

Because these terms are so similar to each other, they often get confused. Even professionals can get a bit confused.

We hope you are getting a sense of how this is a complex area!

Sometimes you will hear people talk about 'autistic features'. We don't like this term because it does not really mean anything. It gets used to describe some of the behaviours that *all* people (children and adults) have that are more commonly seen in those with autism. The problem with the term is that we all have things that might be called 'autistic features'. We both have certain things that we have to organise or do in a certain way, otherwise things feel wrong to us – but, as far as we know, neither of us is autistic.

So, let's get back to talking about autism.

What might autistic children struggle with?

We generally think about autism as difficulties with:

- social communication and social interaction

- rigid and inflexible interests, behaviour and routines.

We know, though, that there are other areas that children with autism may struggle with, or where they might have differences in how they do things or process information compared with 'neurotypical' children.

There can be big differences in the way that autistic children process sensory information. Parents often talk about their children having 'sensory difficulties' or 'sensory processing difficulties' and these can cause some very tricky problems for a child with autism. So, we're going to add this in as an additional area of possible difficulty in autism:

- difficulties with sensory processing.

We also want to flag up anxiety. Anxiety in autism is generally linked to difficulties with rigid and inflexible interests, behaviour and routines, and sensory processing, and we know that anxiety can be a big area of difficulty for children with autism, so we're going to add this in too:

- anxiety.

We are aware that we are already talking about 'difficulties'. We want to say again that it might be just as easy for us to talk about 'differences' rather than 'difficulties'.

Autistic children may struggle with:

- social communication and social interaction
- rigid and inflexible interests, behaviour and routines
- sensory processing
- anxiety.

Autism as a spectrum

Children with autism tend to show certain patterns of behaviour. However, it's really important for us to say that because autism is a spectrum, it is quite possible for a group of children who all have a diagnosis of autism to have very little in common with each other except that they all have a diagnosis of autism.

Autism as a spectrum is a little bit of a simple way to see it, because there are different aspects of behaviour that contribute to the diagnosis and a child with autism can have different levels of each of these aspects of behaviour.

We want to help you visualise what autism as a spectrum actually means and why two children with autism might have very different difficulties. Figure 1.1 shows a picture with two baskets of balloons, with each balloon showing one aspect of autism – we know there are many aspects but we have chosen four:

- social communication and social interaction

- rigid and inflexible interests, behaviour and routines

- sensory processing

- anxiety.

What we hope the picture shows is that for any child, each of these aspects of autism can be at a different level. So, although two autistic children might both have difficulties with social communication and social interaction, rigid and inflexible interests, sensory processing and anxiety, these might be at different levels.

Both children have the same *areas* of difficulty – the same balloons in their basket if you like – but they don't necessarily find the same things equally difficult and so may come across very differently to adults.

Figure 1.1: Aspects of autism

Let's go back to the main areas of difference or difficulty in autism and explore them one by one.

Social communication and social interaction

Social communication and social interaction go together, so we're going to think about them as one big area of difficulty or difference.

When someone's social communication and social interaction is a little different it can have a knock-on effect on their social relationships. For younger children, this might mean a really wide variety of things like:

- struggling to play with others

- struggling to share a game with others or tolerate other people in their play

- struggling to let another child shape or change the game

- not acknowledging other children.

For other children, it can mean really wanting to play with others but not being able to manage it without things going wrong.

Things can go wrong in play for a lot of reasons. Adults often think that it is language that gets in the way, but if you have ever taken a child on holiday to another country, you'll know that even children who speak different languages can just get on and play together – so it is not about language.

Confusingly, an autistic child's relationships with adults, and their ability to relate to adults, may appear very good. This is generally because adults are good at structuring interactions with children and going with what the child wants, while other children may not be so tolerant. Adults are, generally speaking, much more socially skilled than children and so the way in which they make allowances for a child whose social interaction skills are different can cover up the fact that there is any problem at all.

For some autistic children, their difficulties with social communication and social interaction can mean that they are very over-familiar with adults who they don't know, almost as if they don't understand what a trusted adult is. This means that they may be over-familiar and may talk to anyone they meet as if they know them or may make physical contact with unfamiliar adults, for example hugging strangers. This is obviously very risky.

> Children with autism might come across very well to adults – as if they have no difficulties – but they can really struggle when interacting with children of their own age.

Some children get by when they are younger, but it is only when they are older that difficulties with social interaction really start to be noticed. The difficulties that can be noticed include things like:

- retaining an interest in something that others have grown out of and not understanding that other children the same age no longer share this interest

- only wanting to talk about a fixed set of things

- struggling to maintain friendships.

There are many ways that social communication and social interaction can vary. We can all recognise when someone's social communication and social interaction skills are 'different' and we can all recognise that this can feel strange. It can be very hard though to put your finger on what it actually is that is different or what is making the interaction feel different. It might be that someone does not look at you when they are talking to you or they look too intently. They might stand too close or use gestures in a different way (perhaps using too much gesture or none at all). Or it could be someone who only wants to talk about one particular issue and does not notice that you are not interested in what they are talking about. It could also be that they struggle to have a two-way conversation with you.

Social communication and interaction includes:

- spoken words and how they are used

- tone of voice

- body language

- how gestures are used

- seeing another person's point of view

- understanding empathy.

Let's unpick these key areas of social communication and social interaction a little more.

Spoken words

The range of spoken language in autism is really varied and we'll try to give you a flavour of this.

Some children with autism do not have spoken language and appear not to have any clear ways to communicate with others. We know that there are children without autism who, for various reasons, don't have language and these children use other methods of communication, but autistic children without spoken language will still have problems with the other aspects of their communication. They might develop ways of getting their needs met, but their communication will still be different.

Autistic children who do have spoken language really vary.

- Some will have spoken language but do not use it to communicate; they *can* speak and know some words but do not use them to communicate with other people. They may also use their words in ways that don't make much sense to adults, for example they may say only certain words or just use phrases that they have heard elsewhere, such as on a television programme.

- Some children with autism do use words to communicate with others but only use a restricted range of words and may use them in an unusual way. Their language skills may sometimes appear 'scripted'. What this means is that they tend to use the same kinds of phrases to deal with certain situations. These might be phrases that they have picked up from the television or other people or ones that get a specific response from others. Their language might sound okay until you realise that they always use the same phrases.

- Other autistic children have what seems to be typical language at home but do not speak at all in other places; this is known as 'selective mutism'. Not all children who show selective mutism have autism – it's a bit of a complicated area, but you may have a child with selective mutism so we think it's important to mention it.

- Some children with autism can be very literal in how they understand language. This means that they tend to take the words at face value without really understanding the meaning. For example, if they heard someone say, 'You are making me tear my hair out,' then they may actually think that the person is pulling out their hair because they do not understand that it is a turn of phrase or a saying and the person does not mean what the words actually mean. This might sound like a small thing, but it can cause real difficulties for an autistic child because so much of our communication uses metaphors or sayings that can easily be misinterpreted. As adults, we often do not realise how literal we can be.

- Other autistic children appear to use language in much the same way that typically developing children do, until you start to look more closely, and these children can present a real conundrum to adults. For these children, when we suggest to parents that a Speech and Language Therapist might get involved, they often tell us that their child does not have a problem with speaking.

For this last group of autistic children with very high-level language skills, it is difficulties with how they *use* their language that can lead to problems. Sometimes it is the meaning that they attach to certain words that is subtly different from the way that others understand the same words. It is impossible for adults to check out the meaning of every word, but knowing that there can be a lack of shared understanding is incredibly helpful when things do go wrong. This tends to be more of a problem for children who appear to be bright.

Let's take an example of a bright, verbally able autistic girl who is 11. She uses words that adults think they understand, but in fact the meaning she gives these words is subtly different.

- Let's assume she gets highly anxious but does not describe this feeling by using the word 'anxious'.

- She does understand what the word 'anxious' means but she uses the words 'wrong' or 'scary' to describe this feeling.

- If an adult asks her if she is feeling anxious she may not answer in the way they expect and may even say that she does not feel anxious.

This might seem to be a small difference, but often with autism it is the subtle differences that we are talking about. The girl saying that she doesn't feel anxious when she actually does is only going to be confusing to an adult because they can see that she looks anxious. If an autistic child and an adult don't share a common vocabulary then it becomes really hard to work out when things are, or are not, going right.

> It can be useful to know that there might be a lack of shared understanding – just because the words are the same, it doesn't mean they have the same meaning for everyone.

Tone of voice
As well as what words we use, how we use those words in speech is important.

- Children with autism can sometimes speak in a very 'flat' or monotone way, almost as if they are not adding any expression to their words.

- Autistic children can also have trouble matching the tone of their voice (or the volume) to the setting. This can get them into trouble when they have been told to 'Keep your voice down.' They may think that they are doing this but there might not be any noticeable difference for the adult who has asked them to talk more quietly.

Body language and gestures
Body language is an important part of our communication. Most children learn to match their body language to their mood or the situation, but some children struggle with it because the rules are quite subtle and it takes time to learn them.

- Sometimes autistic children can have body language that feels a bit too much or over the top.

The use of gesture is another area where things can 'feel' a little bit different.

- Some children with autism can use very big gestures or may not use them at all. Not using gestures can really get in the way of communication with others because it is a fundamental part of what we do when we communicate. As a little experiment, try having a conversation about something important or interesting whilst keeping your hands by your sides. It's not easy and the person you are talking to will definitely notice that something is different.

Having communication that is different can lead to difficulties in relationships with other people.

For children with autism there can also be difficulties with social relationships that are not just due to differences with language and communication. These can include finding it difficult to see another person's point of view.

Difficulty seeing another person's point of view

We know that autistic children can struggle with 'theory of mind' – this means that they struggle to put themselves in someone else's shoes and so cannot easily understand another person's point of view. (Putting yourself in another's shoes is a lovely illustration of what we were talking about before – how language can be confusing because we are obviously not talking about actually putting somebody else's shoes on!)

Theory of mind can be a little hard to explain so let's use an example:

- If I show a child a Smarties® tube and ask them what is inside they will usually say that it contains Smarties®. If I open it up and show them that it contains stones and ask them again what is inside the tube, they will usually now tell me that it contains stones. If I then say that I am going to invite another child into the room and ask that child what is inside, most will predict that the other child will say the tube contains Smarties®.

- A child with autism is likely to say that the new child coming into the room will predict that the tube contains stones. This is because although *they* know it contains stones, their difficulty with putting themselves in another person's shoes means that they struggle to understand that another person can hold a different view to them, so they struggle to understand that the other child does not already know the tube contains stones.

In terms of relationships with other people, a difficulty seeing another person's point of view (putting yourself in another's shoes) means that an autistic child may struggle to understand:

- what others are feeling and why

- why other people are reacting in a certain way

- that someone else is feeling something different from what they are feeling – this links to problems with empathy.

Differences in understanding empathy

Children with autism can have difficulties with empathy. There are a few different things that contribute to this. Empathy is about understanding what another person might be feeling and why. Difficulties with empathy can work both ways. Some children with autism appear not to have a very good understanding of other people's feelings, but other autistic children can appear to get very upset when other people express emotions, almost as if they feel others' emotions too strongly.

For both of these it is likely that they:

- are struggling to understand what the other person is doing – the other person may look different if they are upset/angry etc. and the child with autism may not understand why, and this may make them feel uncomfortable

- may not have shared the emotional experience that has led to the other person being angry/upset etc.

- may not understand what it is that has happened to make the other person react in this way.

Let's use an example: An autistic child who is not angry may struggle to understand why someone is angry with him, because he cannot put himself in that other person's shoes. Part of the complexity of autism means that even if that other person *looks* angry, a child with autism may not recognise this because he struggles to 'read' other people's expressions and behaviour.

One of the things that can cause extra problems for autistic children is that a bright autistic child can say in *theory* what another person might feel in a given situation but may not be able to apply that theory in *practice*. For example, after an incident he might be able to say that another child was upset by something that he did, but in the heat of the moment he might repeat the same behaviour again, leading to the same outcome.

This can be really difficult for adults to understand, because it looks like the child is choosing to repeat behaviour that they 'know' is wrong. An autistic child may know it is wrong *in theory* but putting it into practice can be a very big problem, especially when the adults around them make the wrong assumptions and see the child as 'choosing' to misbehave.

Through all our clinical work with children with autism, it is when adults see a child as 'choosing' to behave in ways that cause difficulties that problems arise, especially in school. It is important to remember that theory and practice are very different things.

> Knowing what you should do (the theory) and actually doing it (the practice) are not the same thing.

Rigid and inflexible interests, behaviour and routines

Rigid and inflexible interests, behaviour and routines can cause real difficulties for autistic children.

Children with autism have a need for things to be exactly the way they want them to be. We think of it as an area of difficulty because this need for things to be a certain way can get in the way of everyday life. Let's look at some examples to illustrate why this need for sameness can cause difficulties.

- A need for food to be in a certain place on the plate, perhaps not touching any other food.

- Only eating a restricted range of foods – often ones with predictable textures (we'll talk about sensory issues later on).

- Having to have the table settings in a certain place.

- Having a fixed interest in 'niche' things – this can be things like cars, bus routes etc. but can also be things like appearance and make-up. The key thing is that it is a *rigid* and *inflexible* interest.

- Needing to perform specific routines, like touching things in a certain order and having to go back to the start if this sequence is interrupted.

- A real difficulty coping if things that are important to them have changed – the key here is that these are important things to the child, even if they may not seem that way to other people. A good example here might be the ways that their books are arranged on their bookshelf.

- The difficulty coping tends to be out of all proportion to what a casual observer would see as reasonable.

Rigid and inflexible interests, behaviours and routines include:

- a lack of flexibility – needing things to be a certain way and struggling if they are not

- rigid or fixed interests – having an intense interest in something that is unusual, or not appropriate for the child's age, and being preoccupied with that interest

- routines – needing to have or do things in a certain way and *having* to do them.

Lack of flexibility

A lack of flexibility can lead to real difficulties when the child's need for things to be a certain way bumps up against a situation where they cannot do the thing that they need to do.

We are talking about what the child 'needs' to do. We've deliberately chosen this word because we think it is a really helpful way to understand why some autistic children can have so many difficulties doing what adults expect them to. Sometimes their need for sameness and the level of anxiety they feel are so strong that they literally do 'need' to behave in a certain way.

We know that children with autism tend to have a rigid approach to the world, dislike change and want things the way they want them, struggling more than other children to cope when this is not the case. This is the 'rigid' aspect of rigid and inflexible interests and routines.

Restricted or fixed interests

Restricted or fixed interests tend not to cause the same level of difficulty as a general lack of flexibility but they can get in the way of getting on with other children. As we said earlier, the interest that the child has may be shared by other children, but when those children move on to other interests, and the child with autism doesn't, this can be tricky.

We also know that autistic children may have interests that are different from those of other children their age, but even when their interest is shared with others, the child with autism can have an overly intense interest in it.

- Having such an intensity to their special interest so that, for example, they can only talk about this and nothing else can result in other children finding it 'too much'.

- Sometimes interests may start off being shared interests but then other children move on to other interests and the autistic child does not; a good example is Thomas the Tank Engine, where it is typical for young children to be fascinated and even a little obsessed with Thomas, but it is quite a different thing when we are talking about a 12 year old.

In much the same way, a girl who appears to be obsessed with her appearance might be seen as fairly typical until that obsession starts to interfere with everyday life. This interference might be because she needs to get up at 5 am to make sure that her hair and make-up are exactly right. To the untrained eye, her appearance might be just like many other girls of her age, but the fact that it has taken three hours to achieve, and that she may have had to start again two or three times to get it exactly right, may not be typical. We'll talk more about girls in Chapter 2.

Routine
There are a lot of examples of the types of routines a child with autism may show.

A child with autism who has specific routines *has* to perform the routine – if he is interrupted he will generally need to go back and start again so that he can run the routine all the way through. For example, a child who has a routine of touching every door handle on his journey through a space *has* to do this. Similarly, a child who needs to flap his hands and jump up and down when feeling a certain way *needs* to do this otherwise everything will feel wrong for him and there will be a high likelihood of him not being able to cope.

When the routine is more about a *need for things to be a certain way* (for example, when food has to be a certain way on the plate) then his reaction to it not being right can be very extreme and can appear to be out of proportion to what has happened.

Whilst some routines do not get in the way of everyday life, others do, and these can cause real difficulties when the child needs to do them but the situation they are in means that they cannot. This is likely to cause a problem in a school setting or when the adult they are with is in a hurry.

> Not all routines get in the way of everyday life, but when they do it is important to understand the child's need to do them.

Sensory processing differences

We know that children with autism can have a whole host of differences in how they process sensory information, and this can cause difficulties.

Sensory processing differences are a relatively recent addition to how we understand autism. When we first started in clinical practice we used to talk about autistic children being sensitive to noise, but we now understand so much more about how autistic children can struggle with all kinds of sensory processing.

We know from our experience of working with children with autism that sensory processing difficulties can cause problems in all kinds of ways. Here are just a few examples:

- finding noises painful or overwhelming

- being frightened or startled by loud noises

- finding that a lot of noise makes them feel anxious

- feeling anxious when there are too many people around them

- struggling to manage when the temperature is too hot or too cold

- finding strong smells aversive

- finding certain textures difficult to cope with – this might be food or clothing

- struggling when clothing is too tight or not tight enough, made of the wrong material or touching a certain part of the body (collars and sleeves in school shirts are often a big problem)

- struggling to get the right feedback about where their body is in space.

Children with autism can have sensory processing differences that mean that they can be under or over sensitive to different things.

It should be obvious why differences in sensory processing might cause problems for an autistic child. Any one of the examples above (and many more) can cause problems. Sensory differences tend to occur together, and this can overwhelm the child's ability to cope. When we put this together with the need for things to be a certain way, and the difficulties that many children with autism have in expressing how they feel in words, then we can see how sensory difficulties can be really difficult for children to manage.

Sensory differences are also not well understood. Schools tend to have rules about wearing the correct uniform, which can cause real difficulties – an autistic child may spend the whole day trying to keep it all together when his shirt collar is irritating him constantly, when he is too hot because he has to wear a blazer at all times and where there are so many people in a small space causing a lot of noise.

Sometimes the sensory differences for children with autism mean that they can use one way of processing information, rather than lots. This might mean that they pay too much attention to the information coming in from one of their senses without realising that this is happening. Some autistic children might also seek out certain sensory experiences to help give them what they need at a given time. This might be called 'sensation seeking', but it is just a way of a child with autism trying to get what he needs – he might be doing this to block out something else or to deal with anxiety.

Many children with autism find that using a 'sensory diet' can be really helpful in keeping them more grounded, calm and ready for what they need to be doing. A sensory diet is simply a way of giving a child all of the sensory experiences he needs during the day. A good Occupational Therapist can design a sensory diet and give advice on how to use it. For some children, it might be introduced at school or by a parent who has noticed that their child 'needs' certain experiences throughout the day to keep him settled. A sensory diet might include having certain experiences, like firm pressure touch, opportunities for movement breaks and so on.

Anxiety

Anxiety is a theme that we will visit a lot at different points in this book because we think it is not well understood in autism and is really important in helping adults understand why some autistic children can struggle so much with everyday things.

We are going to use a couple of different ways to help you to think about anxiety, its effects and how to manage it. We hope one of these will strike a chord with you.

We want to introduce you to the idea of feeling 'just right'. We know that for many children with autism, feeling 'just right' takes much more work than it does for most children without autism. This is for a whole host of reasons. These include the difficulties that autistic children have in working out what others are feeling and working out how what they are doing impacts on other people and the need for things to be a certain way. Autistic children can also struggle to label how they are feeling, and this makes it hard for adults to understand what is going on for them. Even when a child can label his feelings, he may have a slightly different understanding of the words and this may not be clear to others.

Feeling 'just right' for a child with autism takes much more work, and anything that takes more work makes us feel more tired, and when we are tired we struggle even more to feel 'just right'.

Let's go back to thinking about anxiety.

Anxiety is completely normal; in fact, if humans did not experience anxiety then we would probably all have been eaten by predators a long time ago. Anxiety is normal because it gives us our 'fight, flight or freeze' response; this is the automatic response that our bodies have to a threat so that we either run away, stand and fight, or freeze and play dead.

If you think about times when you have experienced anxiety (and there will be many), you will probably remember experiencing some of these things:

- racing heartbeat

- fast and shallow breathing

- sweaty hands

- feeling hot

- butterflies in your stomach

- struggling to understand which way to act.

All of these are normal responses to threat. Your heart beats fast so that you can run away (take flight) or fight, and because your heart is beating fast, your breathing becomes fast.

You feel hot and sweaty because your heart is pumping blood to your big muscles and your body is also trying to lose some of the heat that this generates. You have no need to digest your breakfast if you are about to become some predator's breakfast, so your digestion stops working normally.

All of these are normal responses to a threat, but they become problematic when our brain tells us that there is a threat when, in fact, there is no big threat.

As well as being normal and something that we need, studies show that having a certain level of arousal (and anxiety is a type of arousal) is actually helpful to us in some situations but, when we have too much, our performance suffers.

Because the same thing or situation does not make everyone anxious, it can be difficult to fully understand anxiety in another person. But we know from research, and from what people with autism tell us, that children and adults with autism can feel very anxious in situations where other people feel fine. Often, though, a child with autism cannot label what he is feeling as 'anxiety'. He may instead show anxiety through an increase in rigid and inflexible interests, behaviour and routines.

Anxiety can be a very real but poorly understood difficulty for children with autism; it is generally related to some of the other areas of difference in autism, including sensory processing.

We already know that children with autism have a strong need for things to be a certain way. They need things to be the way they need them to be – they have a strong need for sameness. So, it is perhaps not surprising that they might feel anxious in a lot of everyday situations where the rules are unclear or where other people are not predictable. In fact, many of the differences that autistic children have can impact on anxiety.

Frameworks for understanding anxiety

It can be helpful to have a framework for understanding anxiety, so we're going to give you a couple to think about here. There is no 'right' framework – frameworks are just ways to help you think about what might be going on. The first one we're going to talk about is the concept of a 'threshold', and the second one is the 'window of tolerance'.

THRESHOLDS

One way to think about why feeling anxious might cause problems for a child with autism is to think about the saying 'the last straw'. We all know that there can be times when we are upset by something small that we would normally cope well with. This is generally because this small thing is the last in a series of things that have happened that have overstepped our limit for coping.

This is the idea of a limit or *threshold*. Thinking about thresholds by using the example of a teacup might help here – just bear with us, we promise this will make sense! Thresholds help us to understand why things that people might ordinarily cope with can become big problems.

Imagine an empty cup. Now imagine that the threshold we are talking about is the top of the cup. If you add a small amount of tea to the cup when it is empty, it will not overflow. If, however, the cup is already pretty full (so the amount of tea in it is near to the top – the threshold), then adding the same amount of tea is likely to result in the cup spilling over, with tea going everywhere. We've shown this in Figure 1.2.

We can think about anxiety in the same way. A small event, such as going out for school break-time and knowing that you don't have anyone to play with, may be something that an autistic child can normally cope well with. If, however, they have already had one break-time where there was nobody to play with and had a lesson that they didn't like (something like writing a story using their imagination or working in a group with other children) and there has been a strong smell of lunch from the dining room, then these factors might act like lots of tea making their cup almost full. If we then add in that they need to make the transition from break-time back into the classroom via the busy cloakroom, it might be that this is the final drop of tea that overflows their cup.

Figure 1.2: Teapots and thresholds

Of course, we are not really saying that autistic children are like a teacup, but we do want to illustrate how a relatively small thing can lead to a big problem.

The problem with anxiety and autism is that many of the everyday things that we all take for granted are the very same things that make an autistic child feel anxious. Figure 1.3 shows the way that anxiety can impact on other aspects of autism and how those aspects can also impact on anxiety.

In reality, it is very difficult to work out which bits of the wheel are contributing to an autistic child feeling anxious at any particular time, but they are *all* important and all interact with each other. This is important for adults to try to remember.

If we go back to the underlying features of autism that we talked about earlier on then it is easy to see how difficulties in any one of these areas, never mind the interaction of several difficulties, can lead to a child feeling highly anxious.

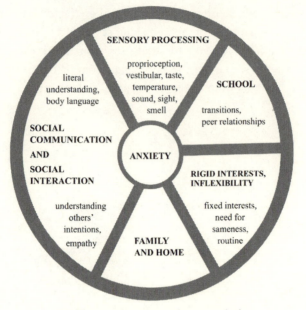

Figure 1.3: The autism and anxiety wheel

WINDOW OF TOLERANCE

This is our second framework. It's a term developed by Dr Dan Siegel, an American psychiatrist, to describe the systems that help people recover from trauma. We're not necessarily using it here to think about trauma right now – we will touch on this in Chapter 7. The 'window of tolerance' helps us to understand how children feel safe.

Many children with autism find the world overwhelming, so understanding what makes them feel safe is important because it helps us to understand when and why they do not feel safe. Not feeling safe and feeling anxious are very similar.

Essentially, the window of tolerance is a way to think about when your child is in their best zone of arousal, so not over-aroused and not under-aroused. Figure 1.4 shows what that might look like.

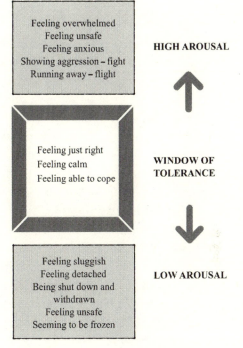

Figure 1.4: The window of tolerance

You don't need to get too caught up in the model in Figure 1.4, because it's the idea of a zone in which things are 'just right' for your child that we want you to understand. We know that Occupational Therapists may say this is similar to how they understand sensory processing. We're also aware that the window of tolerance idea is used a lot when thinking about trauma experienced by fostered and adopted children.

Why can anxiety cause problems?
Let's think for a moment about why children with autism might have difficulties in everyday life. We hope that either the threshold or window of tolerance helps you to understand anxiety.

We have used the example of anxiety to illustrate why there can be difficulties – the wheel that we showed you in Figure 1.3 is intended to show how each of the different areas of possible difficulties in autism can contribute to anxiety and how anxiety can influence each of those areas. You might not have thought anxiety would be so much of a problem in autism, but it really does underpin lots of areas of difficulty.

Of course, children with autism can encounter difficulties with any part of the wheel that have nothing at all to do with anxiety. It can, for example, be very tricky for a child with autism who wants to make friends but whose social skills are not quite at the level that they need to be at to actually make and keep friends.

When your child with autism has very high anxiety, or when her anxiety becomes high in a certain setting, this may indicate that your child is really struggling. Signs of high anxiety might not be obvious but could include an increase in ritualistic behaviour (the *need* to do certain things, an increase in self-stimulating behaviour – sometimes called 'stimming'), repetitive body movements or an increase in meltdowns.

Anxiety can be a sign of general distress in a child with autism and should always be treated seriously. It can also be something that can respond well to making a change in the environment; we'll talk more about making changes in Chapter 3.

What else might be going on?

We know that many autistic children will meet the criteria for another neurodevelopmental difficulty; we are beginning to understand this might be very common and we'll talk about this more in Chapter 2.

We just want to say that for us as Clinical Psychologists, diagnosis is not everything. Clinical Psychologists work with an approach of assessment–formulation–intervention.

Formulation is the way that Psychologists talk about trying to help people make sense of experiences and understand the reasons why they feel or behave the way they do. Although a diagnosis can sit comfortably within that approach, having a diagnosis is not the only way that someone's difficulties can be understood. For autism, understanding the different things that can cause difficulty, how they relate to each other and how they affect the child are far more helpful to understanding how to help than simply knowing that the child is autistic.

Autism and mental health

There can be a real confusion about whether autism is a mental health 'problem' (remember, we don't like the word 'problem' but we're using it here to illustrate a point) or whether autistic children and young people are more likely to have difficulties with their mental health.

Let's deal with the first of these. We've already said that we think that autism has a neurodevelopmental basis, so it's not that helpful to think of it as a psychiatric or mental health problem or disorder. People with autism might get seen in mental health services, but this may be due to the way services are organised rather than what we think autism is.

We know that the ways in which services are organised, and the ways that families access services, are very different across the world. Most of our examples will be about the UK because these are the services we know well, but the point we want to make here is that children with autism may present in either general child health, or in child mental health services.

In the UK, services for children are a little complicated in the way that they are organised – things that adults see as problems with behaviour or emotions might be seen by child health services (such as seeing a Paediatrician) or by Child and Adolescent Mental Health Services (CAMHS) (where the child might see a Psychologist, Psychiatrist,

Nurse, etc.). The way that services are organised means that the same child in different parts of the country might go down either a child health route or a child mental health route.

The second part of this is whether autistic children are more or less likely to have another difficulty that might be seen as a mental health 'problem'. We know that some of the difficulties that come about for someone with autism are the kinds of things that mental health services deal with. Anxiety is the main issue here.

Regardless of why anxiety can be higher in children with autism, having anxiety can be very distressing for a child and his family. Having high levels of anxiety every day, or having high levels of anxiety that are unpredictable, can really get in the way of everyday life. If a child who didn't have autism had high levels of anxiety, they might find themselves being seen in CAMHS services, because we would see high levels of anxiety as something that a mental health service could help with. It is not that simple for children with autism, although we would argue that it should be.

> Mental health problems – including anxiety – for a child with autism are just as distressing as they are for a child who doesn't have autism.

Autistic children with high levels of anxiety are often told that they cannot be seen in CAMHS because 'anxiety is part of autism'. When services say this, they are saying that an autistic child who is experiencing a high level of distress due to anxiety cannot have help from CAMHS but that a child without autism but with the same level of distress due to anxiety can have help. We hope you can see what we think about this. We know that services are stretched, but the evidence from studies tells us that children with autism and anxiety can benefit just as much from help from CAMHS as other children.

Let's introduce some made-up children

We're going to be using some examples of made-up children during this book to try to illustrate some of the points we want to get across. We want to introduce these children here. These are not real children – we have made them up – but the difficulties they are having are very real and we have come across lots of children with very similar difficulties through our clinical work.

Let's introduce Jamil and Emily and explore how autism affects them.

Jamil: a seven-year-old boy who is moving from fostering to adoption

Jamil is a seven-year-old dual heritage boy who lives with his foster parents, Alena and Mark. This is Jamil's second foster placement. His first placement was an emergency one that lasted a few days. Jamil came into care just over a year ago because he experienced neglect and physical abuse when with his birth mum and dad, who struggled with their mental health.

Jamil struggles to understand the subtle social communication and social interaction clues that other children give off. Jamil has loads of language and is really good at using spoken language, so when he communicates with adults he comes across as bright as a button. When he talks to other children though, he tends to stand too close and talks too loudly. At playtime he struggles to play the imaginative games that other children play, and he prefers to run and charge around the playground. He sees other children playing physical wrestling games and, because he's a well-coordinated boy, he runs around grabbing other children during breaktime. The other children don't like this, so they tend to avoid Jamil. This makes Jamil feel really anxious, as he wants to fit in but doesn't really know how to. When Jamil interacts with other children he already finds it hard to work out what they think or what they want to do. So now, when he goes near them, they move away. Jamil is really confused by this.

Figure 1.5 shows Jamil's aspects of autism if we imagined them as being like our basket of balloons.

Jamil really likes to know what is going to happen when. He finds the way that other children sometimes behave when he goes up to them really confusing. Jamil struggles to move easily between charging around at break-time and coming into class again after having lined up.

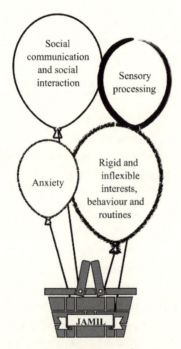

Figure 1.5: Jamil's aspects of autism

It doesn't help that the Teacher tells the class to 'line up smartly' at the end of break-time. Jamil's foster parent tells him that 'looking smart' involves having your shirt tucked in and your hair combed, but all that charging around at break-time has not done anything for the cleanliness of Jamil's school uniform. He doesn't understand how he can 'line up smartly' when he is not looking smart. Jamil's Teacher often comments that he looks as though he has been 'dragged through a hedge backwards'. Jamil hasn't been anywhere near the hedge, so he doesn't understand what the Teacher means. It's very confusing for him.

When Jamil finally gets into class, he is struggling to process all that has gone on. Other children are also crowding the cloakroom, and this makes Jamil feel overwhelmed, both because people are too close to him and it's too noisy. He also isn't sure what is happening. Other children bang into him and, because Jamil doesn't understand this, he thinks they have done it on purpose, which makes him feel even more confused.

Emily: a 12-year-old girl who lives in a foster placement with no immediate plans to move

Emily is a 12-year-old, white, British girl who has been living with her foster parent, Mary, and two other foster children for the past year. Emily first went into foster care about four years ago, when she was eight, because her birth mother used drugs and alcohol and Emily was not well cared for. When Emily lived with her birth mum, they moved house a lot, which meant Emily attended different schools and missed a lot of school. Emily often looked dirty and was hungry. She saw a lot of domestic abuse between her birth mum and birth mum's partners.

Emily's first foster placement was an emergency one that lasted about a month. Emily moved to a second foster placement and stayed there for a few months while plans were made. Emily moved to live with her aunt and cousins, and it was thought that Emily would stay there but her aunt became seriously unwell. Emily had to return to foster care after about two years. She was placed with Mary. Mary is able to offer Emily a long-term placement.

Emily can get on really well with the younger children in her foster home. This has been the case in all her placements, but she struggles much more with people her own age. She struggles to get on with them at school too and is often in trouble at school for what the school call 'making the wrong choices'. This was how things were at primary school too, but she went to several different primaries so her difficulties with getting along with other children her age weren't so clear. She's been at her current school for a full year and it's becoming clear that she is struggling socially. She's struggling to keep friends and is starting to isolate herself at break-times or hanging out with children who seem to enjoy getting her into trouble.

We've shown Emily's aspects of autism in Figure 1.6 – you will see that they are different from Jamil's.

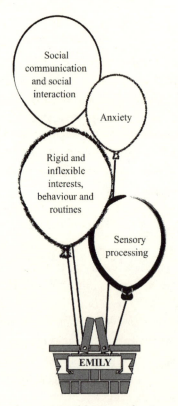

Figure 1.6: Emily's aspects of autism

So, now that we've introduced you to our two made-up children, let's take a moment to summarise what we have covered in this chapter.

SUMMING UP

- Autism is considered to be a neurodevelopmental difficulty.

- Autism needs to be properly assessed by professionals with the right training.

- Children with autism have differences or difficulties with:

  - social communication and social interaction

  - rigid and inflexible interests, behaviour and routines

  - sensory processing

  - anxiety.

- Children with autism do not necessarily have difficulties; being different from other people is not a difficulty.

- Autism is a spectrum, so two children with autism may have very little in common with each other.

- Every child with autism and their family is unique, so there are no right and wrong answers.

- Children with autism can have sensory processing differences that mean that they can be under or over sensitive to different things.

- Anxiety can be a very real but rarely understood difficulty; it is generally related to some of the other areas of difference in autism, including sensory processing.

- A child with autism might also have another co-occurring diagnosis.

Chapter 2

How is Autism Assessed?

Introduction

In this chapter, we're going to look at how autism is assessed, how this might happen and who might do it. We'll also look at some of the other difficulties that might be explored during an assessment.

How common is autism?

You might have heard that people think that autism is on the increase. Nobody is really sure if this is the case, but we are certainly recognising more of it, and this might be because professionals are getting better at recognising what might lie behind some people's difficulties. The definition of what autism is *has* changed over time and this might also have contributed to more people receiving this diagnosis.

It's difficult to reliably estimate how many people have a particular diagnosis. A study in 2014 by Russell and her colleagues suggests that 1–1.7 per cent of children in the UK have been told they are autistic. This means that there are around 1–2 autistic children in every 100 children.

A little note on girls and boys

We can't talk about what autism is without saying something about the differences between girls and boys.

Autism has always been thought of as something that mainly affects boys, and we used to think there were about four times as many males with autism than females. Our understanding has changed though, and we now realise that the idea that four times as many males than females have autism isn't right. It may just be that boys are more likely than girls to get a diagnosis of autism; there can be many reasons for why this might be the case, and we are starting to understand that autism might look different in girls. It is likely that in the future professionals will be better at recognising it in girls, but it can still be problematic to recognise autism in some girls.

Part of the problem is that autism might be more obvious in boys and this has meant that the criteria that we use to diagnose autism are more likely to lead to boys getting a diagnosis. We'll talk about the criteria for diagnosis later on, but essentially these are a set of things that a child has to show or have difficulties with.

We are beginning to realise that girls may have been underdiagnosed in the past because they are a lot better at hiding their difficulties or are just better at managing them. For example, a girl who has an obsession about her appearance and make-up might not be seen as being that different from other girls because the rigid and inflexible interest (or obsession) with make-up is more socially acceptable than, for example, a rigid obsession with trains. Girls also tend to fall out with each other more than boys do, and so difficulties with social relationships might be more hidden in girls or only be recognised later on. This might be what is happening for Emily, who we introduced you to at the end of the last chapter.

Autism might look different in boys and girls.

Neurotypical vs. disorder

We've already talked a little about whether autism should be considered a disorder or not, and we just want to mention that there is a whole range of opinion on this. Some people argue that the strengths that many autistic people have mean that it is not helpful to see it as a disorder, but rather as part of a spectrum of neurodiversity.

We just want to mention this because we think there is much for us to learn about autism that goes way beyond it being considered a disorder. We also like how this focus on neurodiversity suggests a focus on the child rather than the disorder, and we are all for that!

Changing definitions over time

We've talked a little bit about language and some of the different terms that are used for autism. Part of the reason why there are so many different terms around is because there are two sets of diagnostic criteria that professionals might use. These get revised over time, which means that terms from older versions of the criteria might still be being used. The words used to describe autism in these criteria also change over time.

The different terms used to describe autism over the years get absorbed into the language that professionals use, and this is another reason why there are so many words used to talk about autism. Professionals also like to use specific words to describe specific things, but these can get changed by families and so they become less precise.

Some terms for autism also appear to be more acceptable – 'Asperger's syndrome' is one example. Some parents might use it because it sounds less severe than 'autism'. This is one of the reasons that has led to the term 'Asperger's syndrome' being taken out of the DSM criteria. We talk about the DSM criteria a little later on.

PDA

We feel we should talk about PDA here – we need to talk about it somewhere and here feels as good a place as any.

PDA is shorthand for Pathological Demand Avoidance – also sometimes known as Pathological Demand Avoidance Syndrome. If you know anything about PDA, you'll know it's controversial. Most professionals recognise that some children can be extremely avoidant, but it is recognised as part of the autism spectrum rather than a syndrome or diagnosis in its own right.

PDA is a term first used by the late Psychologist Elizabeth Newson to describe children who initially looked like they might be autistic but were highly avoidant of demands; the avoidance was so extreme that it was called 'pathological'. A child who is extremely avoidant of demands will struggle to accept any direct request to do something – even something as straightforward as being asked to sit on the carpet at school, put their shoes on or do a classroom task. All children can be demand avoidant at times, but autistic children who are *extremely* demand avoidant can find it almost impossible to follow any reasonable request when it is asked in a certain way. Children with this kind of demand avoidance can do what adults want them to do when the request is indirect (for example, 'I wonder if you can do numbers one to five on this worksheet'), but not when adults ask directly (for example, 'You need to do numbers one to five').

Things have moved on and we now understand that PDA is part of autism, but it describes children with autism who are *extremely* avoidant of demands. One way of understanding this is that they have such high levels of anxiety that they are unable to comply with reasonable demands placed on them.

PDA is part of autism, but we recognise that children who are extremely avoidant can be extremely challenging.

We have both worked with autistic children who are extre-mely avoidant and we know that these children can be extremely challenging both for parents and school. Parents of these children may say that their child has PDA but, because we have a strong belief in formulation, we don't feel a need to have a separate category of diagnosis for these children. We also recognise that current research does not support PDA as being a separate thing in its own right.

Diagnostic criteria

In order to have a diagnosis of autism, a child has to meet one of the two sets of criteria that are in use, which are the:

- International Classification of Diseases (known as ICD)[1]

- Diagnostic and Statistical Manual of Mental Disorders (known as DSM).

ICD tends to be used in the UK and Europe; DSM is American but is also used in the UK. The two sets of criteria are subtly different, and, just to add to the confusion, they get updated at different times.

We don't want you to get bogged down in the different criteria; it's not possible to diagnose your own child by looking at the criteria – a much more thorough assessment is needed by trained professionals. We have decided not to include the criteria here, but you can easily find them on the internet.

The ICD and DSM use slightly different words to talk about autism.

---

1   The latest version of the ICD criteria, which will be known as ICD-11, is about to come out. At the time of writing this book it had not yet been published and the ICD-10 criteria are the criteria that are in use.

- ICD-10 uses the term 'pervasive developmental disorder' as the group of difficulties that autism falls into. This grouping includes a number of different diagnoses, but the ones that are relevant here are 'childhood autism', 'atypical autism' and 'Asperger syndrome'.

- DSM-5 uses the term 'autism spectrum disorder' and includes three levels of severity.

How is autism assessed, and what is good and poor practice?

Autism isn't really the thing that should be being assessed – it is the child, and her strengths and any difficulties she might have, who should be assessed. As Clinical Psychologists, we always try to hold the child and her family at the centre of our work and, when we do this well, we are assessing the child, not the autism.

We know that people talk about 'diagnostic assessments' but we think this is unhelpful. Any assessment should be aimed at reaching an *understanding* of what is going on for the child and what is causing a problem, rather than looking for a diagnosis. Part of reaching this understanding might be a diagnosis but this shouldn't be the aim of the assessment.

> Assessments should be of the child and family, not just focused on a diagnosis.

Assessment and formulation

Clinical Psychologists work with an assessment–formulation–intervention framework. In this framework, an assessment leads to a formulation, which then guides what any intervention might be. We'll talk about assessment–formulation–intervention throughout this book, but the point we want to make is that the assessment is the thing that leads to the formulation; a diagnosis might sit in there somewhere, but it should not be the aim of the assessment. *Understanding* the child should be the aim. We've illustrated this in Figure 2.1.

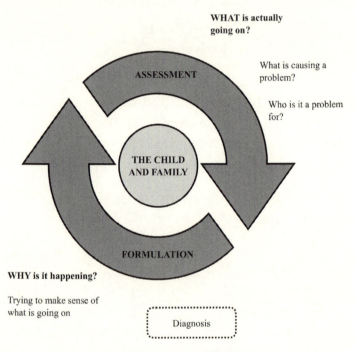

Figure 2.1: Assessment and formulation

We know that in the real world an assessment might lead to a diagnosis, but we want to help people to understand that having some kind of formulation is always going to be important and helpful.

> Consider this: Knowing your child has autism is less helpful than knowing she has sensory difficulties and significant peer relationship difficulties, both of which can lead to high levels of anxiety.
>
> She might not have so many problems with rigid and inflexible behaviour. A diagnosis of autism does not

always tell you what your child's actual differences and difficulties are.

Remember our balloons from Chapter 1 – it's more helpful to know how the balloons look in relation to each other and less helpful to just know that there are some balloons. Here's a reminder of the balloons in Figure 2.2.

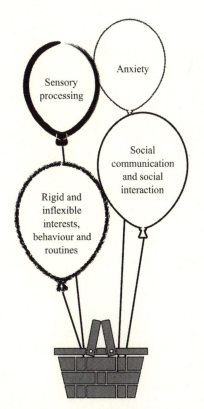

Figure 2.2: Aspects of autism

Having a formulation is much more helpful for predicting where there might be problems and knowing what things to put in place to minimise those problems. Just knowing that your child has autism doesn't really help in predicting where she might struggle but knowing that there are particularly big difficulties with anxiety and sensory processing are aspects of the formulation that might be really helpful. For example, if we think about our made-up girl, Emily, knowing that she struggles socially with girls her own age and that she shows her anxiety by isolating herself at break-times means adults can explore how to make this easier for her.

Understanding what is going on and why – a formulation – will help in understanding what your child may struggle with.

The reality of assessment

We know that in the UK there can be very long waiting times for assessment through the NHS, and families in other countries may also experience delays in assessment. The National Autistic Society has been lobbying parliament about this because children can wait as long as one to two years for an assessment. We think this is a really big problem because of the following reasons.

- Taking this long to make an assessment means that it is one to two years of adults not understanding what is going on for a child. It can mean that a child might have made the transition across several year groups or from primary to secondary school before adults really have a full understanding of the child's strengths and difficulties.

- A delay in understanding the child can get in the way of the child flourishing at school and home. This is a real problem and means opportunities for learning can be lost.

- For some children, especially those with autism who are also extremely demand avoidant, it can mean that they might have been excluded from school or removed from school by parents because no one has been able to understand what is going on. It can also mean many changes in care placements because a child's needs and difficulties have been misunderstood by adults. Sadly, we know that these things happen a lot.

- Assessments taking years to complete also means that parts of the assessment might be out of date before other parts have even begun. If our aim in assessing a child is to understand that child, then having assessments that are out of date can only be unhelpful.

We have both worked in the NHS and we fully understand the pressures that exist there, but one to two years in the life of a child of ten would be the same as 10–20 per cent of that child's life. We wouldn't expect adults to wait for that percentage of their life to get an assessment, so it's quite a mystery why commissioners of services would think it's acceptable for children.

It is tempting to think that we might just do quicker assessments, but these carry their own risks. We know many families who have got as far as seeing a health professional for example, only to be told that their child cannot be autistic because they could hold a good conversation with an adult, and so further assessment has not happened. For girls, there can be particular problems because quick assessments can lead the professional to say that the child is 'too sociable' to have autism. These quick assessments are not the kind of multidisciplinary and thorough assessments that we think children should be having.

It is a difficult balancing act, but one that we need to get right.

We need the right balance of assessments that don't take too long but are good enough.

Where might assessments happen?

An assessment of a child might happen in different places. We are going to talk mainly about the UK here, but the principles should be the same across other countries. The UK has a National Health Service (NHS), which is free at the point of need for anyone to access, but in other countries a family may need the right kind of health insurance to access assessment.

Normally, when a parent starts to notice that a child is struggling, the first port of call is the General Practitioner (in the UK this is the child's GP but in other countries this might be the primary care physician). The GP might want to watch and wait for a while, but at some point a referral will be made to someone who can take a closer look. In the UK, this is normally all done within the NHS and the referral is generally to a Paediatrician or to a CAMHS. In other countries there may be different referral routes and different services that might be involved – your primary care physician will be able to tell you.

Sometimes there are other stops along the way. In the UK these might include the School Nurse or an Educational Psychologist (if problems are first noticed in school) or the Health Visitor (for children under five), but because an assessment of a child where someone thinks there might be autism is specialist, it is normally, in the UK, going to end up with a Paediatrician or in CAMHS at some point.

For a fostered or adopted child, the process might be a little different. Again, services in other countries will be different, but in the UK, concerns might first be discussed during their initial LAC (looked-after child) health assessment when they first come into care or at your child's annual LAC health care review meeting. Referrals for more assessments might then be made. Concerns might also be discussed with your child's Social Worker and referred into the health assessment pathway (in the UK, this is the NHS) that way. An assessment might also come via the family court process.

Whichever route your child takes, the assessment is a specialist one because it is complex. You will know from our discussion in Chapter 1 that autistic children can present with very different kinds of difficulties and these need careful assessment. It is considered to be good practice for an assessment to be done by more than one person, again because it is complex. Here are some of the people who might be involved either through CAMHS or the Paediatrician:

- Paediatrician

- Clinical Psychologist

- Child Psychiatrist

- Speech and Language Therapist

- Occupational Therapist

- Educational Psychologist.

There might be other people, but there should generally be a medical doctor and another professional.

> Assessments involve a lot of work and that is one reason why they are normally done by more than one person.

Some children are assessed through a private sector route, and there are many reasons why this might happen. In some countries this is the normal route, and in the UK where there is a national health service, families sometimes don't want to wait for an NHS assessment and are able to afford a private assessment. Other families may have had an NHS assessment and are not happy with it or cannot get a referral to an NHS service because of how the service accepts referrals. In some areas, social services may have their own procedures for arranging health assessments, but your Social Worker will know.

There are lots of different routes into assessment. It all depends on the child, who is concerned and how local services are arranged.

It is important for us to say that schools cannot 'diagnose' autism. A Teacher might say that they think a child may have autism, but Teachers aren't trained to do assessments for autism. Of course, Teachers are really important when an assessment does happen because they see the child for a large part of the day and they can often recognise patterns in behaviour. We know they can give us invaluable information about how the child behaves in a structured setting, with groups, with other children and so on.

Whichever route the child goes down (NHS, education, private sector, court, etc.) the assessment should:

- be multidisciplinary (done by more than one profess-ional)

- be of high quality

- cover a number of different areas.

A good assessment should include the following.

- A developmental history taken from parents, carers or, if this is not possible, people who knew the child when they were very young. We know this can be tricky for some fostered and adopted children. The developmental history part of an assessment around autism is incredibly detailed and takes several hours to complete; it cannot be done in ten minutes and should focus on difficulties that research tells us are seen in autism.

- Observation of the child in a social setting; normally this is in school.

- Individual assessment with the child – this might be done using something like the Autism Diagnostic Observation Schedule (ADOS) but it does not have to be done using any formal approach. A good Speech and Language Therapist, Psychologist, Paediatrician or Child Psychiatrist can do a play-based assessment with a child.

- Discussion with people who know the child well, including information about current concerns from the school.

Figure 2.3 shows what an assessment might look like, from concerns to formulation. This is just an example as we know it won't always look like this.

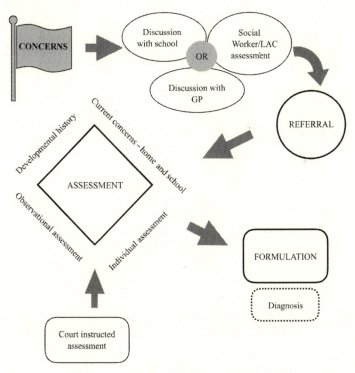

Figure 2.3: How an assessment process might look

We just want to mention here that there are no tests for autism. This might surprise you, but it's true. A diagnosis of autism is based on the diagnostic criteria and the professionals' clinical judgement about whether the child meets different parts of those criteria.

> There are no tests for autism. Different professionals might use questionnaires or play-based assessments, but autism cannot be ruled out or diagnosed based on a questionnaire.

A professional might use questionnaires to find out more information about the child but there are no questionnaires that can diagnose autism. You might come across the ADOS, a play-based assessment that many professionals (including us) use when assessing a child.

Although the ADOS includes the word 'diagnostic' in its name, it cannot diagnose autism. What it can do is help to structure a way of interacting with a child to try and highlight certain behaviours. Worryingly, we do know that some professionals might say that a child 'passed' the ADOS but there is no such thing as 'passing' or 'failing' the ADOS. The ADOS is a play-based assessment and is not meant to be used to 'diagnose' a child.

We'll say it again because we think it is so important: there are no tests that can diagnose autism. Autism is diagnosed based on good clinical judgement after collecting a great deal of information across different settings.

Health, social care and education working together

Our experience over the years has taught us that it is really important for health, social care, education and families to work together with the child at the centre of their thinking.

This might sound easy but in practice it is often very difficult. There are different reasons for this.

The behaviour that the child shows in school can be very difficult indeed for other children, but if it is seen as deliberate misbehaviour by the child, or that the child is 'choosing' to behave in a certain way, this can lead to a view being taken that the child needs a 'behaviour approach' rather than understanding that there might be neurodevelopmental difficulties. When this kind of mismatch between parents and the school occurs, it is very often the case that parents move the child to a different school.

We talked in Chapter 1 about how children with autism can often say what they should do in theory but are not able to put that into practice; this is what is generally happening when a school sees a child as 'choosing' to behave in a certain way. We can understand how this happens – a child who can say what she should have done but repeatedly appears to 'choose' to do the exact opposite can very quickly be seen as making deliberate choices. In our experience, children with autism who are markedly avoidant and very verbally able are most likely to fall foul of this.

For some fostered or adopted children, it could be assumed by professionals that their difficulties with social communication and social interaction have arisen because of experiences of abuse or neglect. Of course, this could be the case, but only focusing on one explanation means that a neurodevelopmental condition like autism may be missed.

Working together and holding the child at the centre of everyone's thinking is *always* good for a child and her family.

Some schools, of course, do a fantastic job, and understand that they are part of a wider system for the child and make fantastic changes to accommodate the needs of a child with autism. These are sometimes really small changes, such as allowing a child to go into the classroom early to avoid the cloakroom crush or do something more structured or special at unstructured times during the day (break-time and lunchtime) when the social demands and unwritten rules can overwhelm a child's ability to manage. We'll talk more about this in Chapter 4.

Social workers can do a great job of pulling together everyone who is involved with your child, including you as her parent, so that information and ideas can be shared. Working together as a team is vital.

Co-occurring difficulties/'comorbidity'

We mentioned in Chapter 1 that autistic children can also meet the criteria for other diagnoses. These might be things like attention deficit disorder (ADD), attention deficit hyperactivity disorder (ADHD), Tourette's syndrome, dyspraxia or developmental coordination disorder to mention just a few. We also know that autism can be associated with a number of known genetic syndromes such as Fragile X syndrome.

We're also beginning to understand the numbers of children who have foetal alcohol spectrum disorder (FASD); we know that there are a lot of fostered and adopted children with FASD and that meeting the criteria for autism can be part of FASD. A lot of children with FASD will also meet the criteria for other neurodevelopmental conditions.

You might wonder why it matters that a child has more than one diagnosis, and very often it doesn't matter, but the thing about diagnoses is that they help adults to predict how a child might behave. If adults know a child has autism then they might expect that child to have difficulties in social communication and social interaction, rigid and inflexible interests and so on. When we add in another diagnosis, it makes it harder for adults to predict how the child might behave.

For example, if a child has autism and ADHD then the adults around him might not really understand his behaviour. This is another reason why we like formulations because they can be used to make better predictions about how a child with, for example, autism and ADHD might behave.

Of course, there are lots of combinations of diagnoses that children with autism may have and other children will only have a diagnosis of autism.

> Children with autism can have another diagnosis too, and it can sometimes be tricky to work out what things are due to autism and what are due to another diagnosis.

To make it even more complicated, children who end up with more than one diagnosis very rarely acquire all those diagnoses at the same time. So, they may get a diagnosis of ADHD but if there are still problems even when this is well managed, they may then go on to get a diagnosis of autism later on. Children also keep developing and moving through year groups and schools and this makes things even more complicated.

For any child with one diagnosis or many, for us as Clinical Psychologists it is the formulation that is key. Knowing that a child struggles with sensory processing, has rigid and fixed interests that mean they need things to be a certain way, is very impulsive and may need specific adjustments made for them in school is really helpful. But, knowing only that they have autism and ADHD is probably less valuable.

Specific issues for fostered and adopted children

We have briefly mentioned that there can be specific difficulties for fostered and adopted children when it comes to assessment. A child growing up in his birth family will have adults who have known him right from the start, who will know all about the pregnancy and birth, his early days, weeks and months, how he behaved at different points, when he developed language and how and so on. All of these things are crucial parts of the developmental history that are part of the assessment process.

For fostered and adopted children, so much of this information may be missing and this can pose a real problem. If nobody holds this very detailed history of the child's development, or if different sets of parents and professionals hold different bits of it, then it's not going to be at all straightforward to collect it all. For some children, it will not be available at all, or will only be available in tiny chunks.

This means that the process of assessment for a child who is fostered or adopted, where there is a suspicion that they may have difficulties that go along with autism, might look very different and last even longer.

Fostered and adopted children are a little more complicated to assess, but all the elements of the assessment should still be possible.

It may be that fostered or adopted children who are being assessed with an eye on whether they might be autistic are likely to have more of the other co-occurring difficulties that we talked about earlier on. We know that for any child where there are co-occurring difficulties (including things like ADHD, FASD etc.), the assessment process is going to take longer, because the professionals doing the assessment will need to tease out what aspects of the child's behaviour might be due to what area of difficulty.

It might also be the case that different teams get involved for different types of difficulty. This may add additional problems and time. In the UK, some NHS services are specialised for assessment of autism and others for assessment of ADHD, and they may not see children who have a mix of different difficulties. This is really unfortunate for any child but even more so for fostered or adopted children, where there might be separate 'looked-after' services that may or may not have the expertise needed around neurodevelopment. Also, if a fostered or adopted child goes through generic CAMHS assessment services, those services might feel they don't have the necessary expertise in fostered and adopted children. This is how it can get even more complicated.

Let's add in the other big issue that's around for fostered and adopted children, which is attachment. We're going to talk about attachment later in Chapter 6, but we want to flag up here that some children with attachment difficulties can appear very much like children with autism, and this starts to make things very complicated indeed. In fact, they can feel so complicated that the child gets caught between different services and different ideas of what might be going on and people might end up no further forward in understanding what might be happening and what might underlie some of the difficulties.

Assessment for Jamil and Emily

Let's now think about our two made-up children – Jamil and Emily – from Chapter 1 and consider their assessment process.

Jamil is seven and is living in a foster home. He's been there for one year and is about to move to an adoptive placement.

Emily is 12 and is living in a foster home. She has lived in a few different homes. She is not about to move again.

For both Jamil and Emily, the fact that they have moved home a few times adds a complication to their assessment process. For Jamil, the fact that he is about to move again adds another obstacle for getting an assessment.

In many areas, services tend to be organised based on geographical areas. In the UK, they are likely to be based on where the child's GP is; this means that when a child moves home, he may move to a different service 'patch' and is no longer eligible to be seen by the service he is currently on a waiting list for. It is not like this everywhere, but in big city areas it can be a real problem when services are organised into 'city' and 'suburb' patches and where moving only a short distance can mean moving service patch. Even if moving house means the child stays in the same patch, he may come under a different education patch and so it is easy to see how this can lead to delays in assessment.

It can be useful to know that in some areas some services have an agreement that if a fostered child is on a waiting list for a service in one area and he then moves to a different area, the time on the previous waiting list will be taken into account. Check this with your child's Social Worker.

Jamil's assessment

Jamil was first referred to the local Paediatrician by his GP when he was five because there were concerns at school about his ability to follow instructions and he was struggling with understanding the social interaction of other children.

The waiting time for seeing the Paediatrician was four months for an initial appointment (we know it is far longer than this in some areas). Once he had waited and seen the Paediatrician, the local NHS autism assessment pathway required him to also see a Clinical Psychologist for more assessment. Jamil moved into care while he was on the waiting list, so the service decided that his assessment should be put 'on hold' until he had settled and his future plan for care became clearer. Jamil was finally seen for an assessment just before a possible match was found for adoption.

Figure 2.4 shows what Jamil's assessment journey might have looked like. We've added some hands to show where the assessment can get stopped or slowed down.

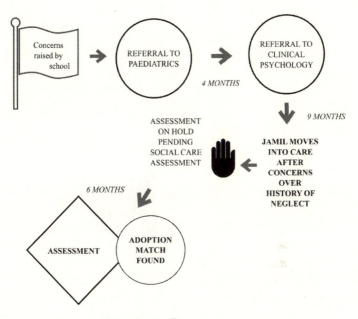

Figure 2.4: Jamil's assessment process

Emily's assessment

Emily has moved home and school several times in her life. During most of her life, there have been a lot of serious concerns about her safety and how well she has been cared for, and these worries led to her going into care. It's only recently that concerns about her social communication and social interaction have been raised.

Her school has concerns about Emily's relationships with other girls and about what they see as emerging 'sexualised behaviour' towards boys. She is also struggling to comply with what Teachers want her to do and is often late for lessons. The school has asked the school counsellor to see her, and has discussed her with its Educational Psychologist. The concerns have also been shared with Emily's Social Worker, but Emily has not yet been referred to anyone outside of the school. We have shown the assessment process for Emily so far in Figure 2.5.

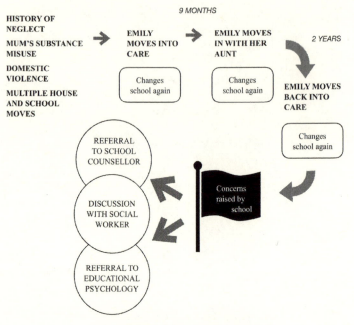

Figure 2.5: Emily's assessment process

We hope you can see from both of these examples that there are lots of places where an assessment can get stuck for a fostered and adopted child and lots of opportunities for information to be missing. We've mentioned how complicated it gets when a fostered or adopted child is being assessed in terms of autism, so information that is missing is a real headache for everyone.

SUMMING UP

- Autism may or may not be more common than it used to be, but we are better at noticing it.

- We are beginning to recognise that autism might look quite different in boys and girls.

- There is some suggestion that we might not see autism as a disorder at all, but just a difference.

- PDA is part of autism, but we recognise that children who are extremely avoidant can be extremely challenging.
- A diagnosis of autism is done in relation to either the ICD or DSM diagnostic criteria.
- Assessments should be of the child and family and not just focused on a diagnosis.
- Assessments involve a lot of work and that is one reason why they are normally done by more than one person.
- There are lots of different routes into assessment. It all depends on the child, who is concerned and how local services are arranged.
- There are no tests for autism.
- Working together and holding the child at the centre of everyone's thinking is *always* good for the child and their family.
- It is *very* common for a child with autism to have another diagnosis too.
- Fostered and adopted children are a little more complicated to assess, but all the elements of the assessment should still be possible.

Chapter 3

Overriding Principles for Parenting a Child with Autism

In this chapter, we are going to do three main things.

- Give you a set of key, overriding principles and help you understand why they are important.

- Talk you through some of the key strategies that you might find particularly helpful for parenting an autistic child.

- Talk you through some tricky situations that you might encounter with your child.

This chapter is not about us giving you a set of 'how to' instructions, because the key theme is getting to know *your* child.

For anyone reading this who is not a parent to a fostered or adopted child, it might seem strange to suggest that someone might need to get to know their child but, really, all parents are in this situation to a greater or lesser degree, because even when you get to know your child as a birth parent, that child keeps changing as they grow, develop and experience new things.

For any child, there can be bumps along the road of development, but for fostered or adopted children, the bumps might be bigger, come earlier and be more disruptive. For a child with autism who is also fostered or adopted, it is so important that she has a parent who understands her.

> Knowing your child and understanding her is going to be more helpful than any parenting or behaviour management advice.

You may have tried other approaches that say how you 'should' approach parenting. What we want to do is to give you some things to think about so that you can reflect on your parenting – what is going well and what is not going so well – and then think about what you want to change or what you have the energy to change. We recognise that many things can impact on parenting, including how much support you have at home, how much support you and your child get from school and social care, and the needs of other children you may be caring for.

One thing we know very well as Psychologists is that it is very hard to make a change when you don't have the necessary things in place to support you with making a change. We'll point you in the direction of other professionals who can be great sources of support and advice in Chapter 9.

> In order to make changes, you will need to feel supported.

Let's introduce you to our overriding principles; we hope you find them helpful.

Principle 1: Know your child (and his autism)

Our first principle is: know your child (and his autism). There are many things that you can do to try to learn as much about your child's autism as you can. Remember that not all children who might get a diagnosis of autism have one, so if your child struggles with social communication and social interaction, or is particularly rigid and inflexible, learning about these aspects of his make-up will be helpful too. There are a lot of ways to gather this information, but the key thing is that it's helpful to understand what helps your child to feel 'just right', what makes him tick and what he finds difficult.

Our checklist

Let's introduce our checklist, which you can find in the Appendix and download yourself. We've included it to remind you of all the things that can be helpful to know about your child and his autism. It can be used at any stage of your journey with your child – before he moves to live with you and once he is living with you (we'll explore this more in Chapter 5).

Remember that when we are thinking about autism we need to think about the core areas. The checklist is designed to help you to work out what these core areas might mean for your child.

We've separated the checklist into different sections to make collecting information more manageable:

- social communication

- anxiety and feeling 'just right'

- social interaction

- rigid and inflexible interests, behaviour and routines

- everyday transitions

- sensory needs.

We've also added a section for you to put the things that help a place be 'just right' for your child.

The checklist isn't something that you have to use. You might already know a lot about your child. Feel free to use it in whichever way works best for you.

Thresholds and the window of tolerance

We introduced you to the idea of thresholds and a window of tolerance in Chapter 1. You'll remember that the window of tolerance is all about your child feeling 'just right' and not being under- or over-aroused; we also illustrated the idea of a threshold with an overflowing teacup. These are important ideas to keep hold of because they will tell you a lot about your child.

Knowing what makes your child with autism anxious, what affects his threshold, and what sensory experiences can calm or overwhelm him are all things that are important to you understanding him. This understanding is a crucial part of helping him to feel safe.

Feeling safe is extremely important to all of us, and it is of vital importance to any fostered or adopted child.

The benefits of getting to know your child are numerous for both of you. When you know and understand your child, it becomes a lot easier to manage behaviours that either you, or your child, may be finding difficult.

> Understanding what makes your child feel 'wrong' or 'not right' is really important. Your child may not be able to label these feelings, so your understanding of what his behaviour may be saying about how he feels is so important.

Principle 2: Get alongside your child

Before we start on our second principle – all about getting alongside your child and being child focused – we want to say that we know that not all professionals who might be involved with your child will agree with what we are going to say here about getting alongside your child. Some professionals may say that the key thing is for your child to fit in to the world the way that everyone else does, but we are firm believers in understanding *your* child, getting to know *him*, and understanding *his* world.

> We think it is more helpful to your child if you understand him and his world, rather than trying to get him to fit in to the world like everyone else does. In our experience, trying to get your child to fit in to the world, without understanding him, is likely to cause distress all round.

What does it mean to get alongside your child?

Getting alongside your child might literally mean getting down on his level or it might mean just taking a moment and thinking, 'What is this situation like for my child?' This last bit can be difficult because the times when you most need to do this are usually the times when you need to be doing other things or when you are trying to stop things escalating to the point where it all goes horribly wrong. But you might want to stop and think about how full his teacup is and why or whether he is in, above or below his window of tolerance. You can also do this kind of thinking after a difficult incident.

Understanding your child is something that develops over time and over different situations. This is not at all straightforward if you are a foster or adoptive parent who has had a new child come to live with you. Often it is only by going through difficult times with your child that you develop your understanding of what things are like for him.

> You will learn about your child over time and possibly only really through times when things go wrong.

The role of play

One of the things that can help in getting alongside and understanding your child is to engage in the to and fro activities that are part of play. This can be a great way of entering your child's world.

We know that children with autism can struggle with this 'to and fro', 'back and forth' element of play, because they struggle to have the same level of understanding about turn taking, social communication and social interaction. But this does not mean that you cannot play with your child if he has autism. Playing alongside him, or letting him lead the play, without trying to direct him or intervene, might be just the thing that you need to do to join him in his world without raising his level of anxiety.

Play serves many functions for all children; adults like to play too. Play for a child with autism may look different, but children with autism still play. Jamil, our seven-year-old made-up boy, likes to play, but he struggles to negotiate successful play with other children because he isn't very good at making up games or playing in an imaginary world. Jamil prefers to charge around because this makes things much more predictable, and he likes things to be predictable.

When Jamil was younger, he liked to play with his cars, lining them up neatly and inspecting the wheels. His mum never liked him doing that and never played with his cars with him. You will remember that Jamil is moving from a foster placement to an adoptive placement and there are many things about the move that are making him feel 'not right'. Recently, he has started to play with his cars in the same way as he did when he was younger.

Figure 3.1 shows us what could happen if Jamil's foster parent tried to intervene in his play and how this might be different from what might happen if she joined his play instead.

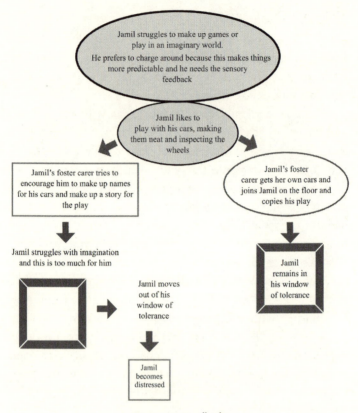

Figure 3.1: Jamil's play

We hope that you can see from Figure 3.1 that what Jamil's foster carer does might have different outcomes for Jamil, where he is in his window of tolerance and his level of distress.

You'll remember from Chapter 1 that children with autism often cannot tolerate anyone else in their play space or interfering with their game. Confusingly for adults, it might look like Jamil is just lining cars up and spinning their wheels rather than playing. There can be a huge temptation to intervene and play 'with' the child, when Jamil might only be able to tolerate someone playing alongside.

Play doesn't necessarily mean interfering with what your child is doing – he may not be able to tolerate you intervening in his play, even if it doesn't look like he is really playing.

We want to be clear that we don't want you to try to make your child's play like that of other, neurotypical children, because children with autism have difficulties with social communication, social interaction and rigid and inflexible interests and routines, while neurotypical children do not. Children with autism can, and do, play but it might look different.

We know that play builds a strong foundation for social interaction (amongst other things) and we also know that children with autism do need to interact in the real, non-autistic world, so being able to tolerate others in their play space and in their play is an important skill.

Understanding this within the context of your child's threshold or his window of tolerance is crucial. For example, knowing that Jamil is likely to hit out when he feels overwhelmed – when his teacup is overflowing or when he is over-aroused and outside his window of tolerance – is crucial information for helping him (and the adults around him) to manage the social interactions that he *will* have at school and other places.

We want you to take opportunities to play with (or alongside) your child, and to join him in his world, but not to push him outside of the zone in which he feels safe.

In some areas, your fostered or adopted child may be able to access play-based therapies, which can help you to join his world and sensitively develop your interaction with him. We want to mention a couple of interventions, called Theraplay® and Lego®-Based Therapy, which are both used with autistic children. Theraplay® is great for helping you to get to know your child and his window of tolerance, while also developing 'to and fro' interaction. Lots of fostering and adoption services offer Theraplay®. Lego®-Based Therapy focuses on developing social skills.

A word about Applied Behaviour Analysis

We want to mention that some interventions are used to try to change a child or get him to be easier to manage. One of these is Applied Behaviour Analysis (ABA) and it's quite controversial. We know that many parents like it, but we don't see ABA as a way to help you get alongside your child.

We are not against trying to shape your child's special interests or his behaviour, but we are definitely against trying to remove behaviours just because adults don't like them. All behaviour happens for a reason but if we don't understand that reason, all that happens is that an autistic child will start to show a different behaviour that serves the same purpose when we try to remove a behaviour that adults don't like. If we try to understand what that purpose is, we can try to 'shape' the child's behaviour by encouraging something that serves the same purpose but is more acceptable or by encouraging the child to display the behaviour only when it is acceptable.

For example, a child may like to be naked and he may take off all of his clothes when he's anxious because this makes him feel safe. Adults find this difficult, for obvious reasons, but if we understand the getting-naked behaviour as the child's attempt to manage his anxiety, then it is easy to see that we can then try to encourage a more acceptable way of managing anxiety that doesn't involve being naked.

Principle 3: Understand the communication in your child's behaviour

In this section, we're going to talk about communication and behaviour, which is our third principle – understanding what your child is telling you or understanding the communication in his behaviour. We are putting commu-nication and behaviour together because, as Psychologists, we understand that children communicate through their behaviour. For children with autism, though, it can be a little harder to work out what is being communicated.

We want you to understand that you are the expert on your child. Other people and professionals may be involved, and they will be experts in some things, but they do not know your child as well as you do – even if your child has only recently come to live with you. It is you who will see him in the most different situations and so you *will* know him better than perhaps anyone else, even if it doesn't feel like it. You will probably be the person who sees the most of your child and sees him in the most situations, and the person who sees his range of responses to different situations.

Understanding what your child is telling you involves some different things. We have already talked about being child focused and developing your understanding of what autism means for your child. Understanding what your child is telling you is crucial because when we understand better how things are for another person, we can adjust our own behaviour and the environment around that person to make a positive change.

Let's go back to our core areas and have a think about some of the things you will need to understand from what your child is telling you. It's going to be most helpful to think about your child when he has struggled with something, because when things are going well it can be tricky to work out why. It is often much easier to look back at a situation where things have not gone well and try to unpick what happened.

One of the ways to do this is to think about the different areas that we know children with autism can struggle with and try to work out if any of them were contributing to the difficult situation. The checklist in the Appendix might help.

So, try to think about a situation that your child has struggled with and consider the following areas.

- Social communication and social interaction.

    – How was your child understanding the situation? Were the rules explicit and understood? Remember that not everyone understands a situation in the same way – you might have a clear idea of what just happened, but your child may not.

    – How was your child communicating in the situation? Remember that if your child has limited language, or does not use language, then his school could be a gold mine in terms of helping with communication aids.

- Rigid and inflexible interests, behaviour and routines.

    – Do you know what the behaviours are that your child *has* to do and the situations where he feels a stronger need to do them?

    – Do you understand what happens when he is not able to do these things? Was that happening here? These behaviours might include him asking repetitive questions, talking about his special interest, showing certain physical movements or doing something in a certain way from start to finish.

- Sensory processing.

    – Was there anything about the situation that might have led to his sensory processing being overwhelmed? Was it too hot, too cold, too noisy or too bright?

- Anxiety.

    – Do you think your child was showing any signs of anxiety? Remember there can be a big overlap between anxiety and rigid and inflexible behaviour and with having to do certain routines.

Principle 3 overlaps with principle 4, which we are going to talk about next.

Principle 4: Look behind your child's behaviour

Let's develop principle 3 into our fourth principle, which is look behind your child's behaviour, which involves thinking about the *what* and *why* of behaviour.

We hope that if you've managed to think about a situation where things did not go so well, you will already be starting to think about the *what* and *why* of behaviour. We've already talked about how understanding this (what we'd call a formulation) is the first step to thinking about what needs to change to make things more manageable.

> Remember that behaviour is about communication

Knowing *what* is a problem, *who* it is a problem for and *when* it is a problem are also going to be important. Your child might be displaying some behaviour that people see as difficult or distressing, but it does not mean that the problem lies *within* your child. It is going to be important to try to work out what his behaviour (such as refusing to do something, being upset, appearing anxious, showing repetitive behaviours, etc.) is in response to. We've given an example of what this might look like in Figure 3.2.

We want to say that we can never really look at behaviour in isolation. Any behaviour that you see (and this can be anything such as laughing, hitting and rocking) results from a complex interaction of lots of different things.

Let's remind ourselves why understanding your child's behaviour is so important.

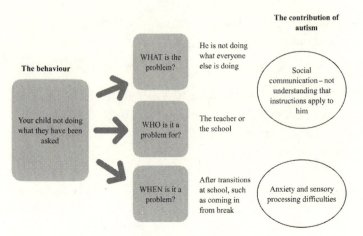

Figure 3.2: Understanding what behaviour is about

Knowing your child means that you will develop a good understanding of:

- *what* his behaviour is actually about – he might be shouting and screaming but he may actually be highly anxious rather than angry

- *why* it might be happening – what has led up to it and what has kept it going.

We know that most parents reading this book will not be Psychologists. You don't need to be one! All you need is to understand the importance of looking *behind* the behaviour to see what might be going on. You are the expert on your child, so you know him better than anyone. This doesn't mean that you will always get it right (remember that none of us gets it right all the time), but it does mean that you have a really good idea about what makes your child tick.

The what

Let's unpick an example of behaviour to see what might lie behind it. We are focusing on understanding *what* is going on.

It might seem strange for us to say that you need to get a sense of what you are looking at, but as Psychologists we know 'behaviour talks loudly'. This means that as adults we tend to look at what a child is doing or showing and then assume that we know what is going on. Let's use our seven-year-old Jamil to illustrate what we mean.

- Jamil hits another child (Lizzie) who has just come into the room very excited and laughing loudly. The adults think that what they are seeing is Jamil being aggressive towards Lizzie for no reason.

Let's unpack this a bit – Jamil did hit Lizzie, that's not in doubt because it was seen to happen – but that is not all that is going on – Jamil had reasons for doing that, even if the adults can't see those. The reasons for hitting are complicated but it is important to understand that they are not always things that have just happened or things that are obvious to people who are watching.

Let's go back to think about Jamil:

- What if Lizzie was showing some kind of emotion before she was hit, and what if Jamil was feeling anxiety because of her display of emotion?

Let's add in some other things:

- What if Lizzie had been very loud the last time she was with Jamil, and what if he has sensory difficulties and is unable to process very loud noise?

- What if Jamil had heard a lot of loud and frightening noises when he lived with his birth parents, prior to foster care?

We hope you are starting to get a sense that what you see is not the full picture. That's why it's important to look *behind* what appears to be happening.

Let's take another example, this time using our 12-year-old Emily:

- Emily is unable to cope with anyone in her room and responds aggressively when anyone touches her possessions.

If we unpack this example, we might find that Emily, who lives in a foster family, has a very significant need for things to be just the way she left them, and she cannot bear the idea that anyone else has touched her things.

Emily has a big collection of Lego®, but it is a collection and not for playing with. She likes to look at the pieces and arrange them in a certain way, but they are not used as toys.

When other children in the foster family touch her Lego®, she will definitely know, even if they think they have put it back just the way it was. Because Emily has autism and has difficulties with social communication and social interaction, she struggles to understand that other children might be jealous of her collection of lovely Lego®, and she struggles to negotiate the difficult interactions that follow when she shouts at them for touching her things.

We hope you are getting a sense that what looks like aggression from Emily is actually a reflection of her difficulties with understanding others' points of view and in negotiating tricky social interactions.

Formulation – the why

Now we have started to look at the *what*, let's think about the *why*. This is what we call the formulation – the word Psychologists use for trying to make sense of what is happening.

If we think about Jamil hitting Lizzie, we already know that it's not as simple as him hitting her for no reason. There wasn't an obvious trigger that adults could clearly see but there were reasons. The reasons are further back in time and relate to Jamil's anxiety, his previous experiences and his sensory processing difficulties.

We can suggest that Jamil found his last encounter with Lizzie stressful because she is very loud. Loud noise makes him feel unsettled and this raises his anxiety. Jamil is unable to understand what is happening to Lizzie's face when she is roaring with laughter. Jamil's response to overwhelming anxiety is to hit because this produces a predictable response, which is him being removed from the room. When Jamil is removed from the room, the noise level drops and he is on his own. His anxiety drops.

In this situation, Jamil has a good outcome because the noise level has gone down, and he does not need to worry about what might happen because it has already happened – he has been removed from the room.

Figure 3.3 shows what this process might look like.

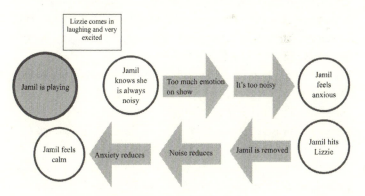

Figure 3.3: Jamil and Lizzie

Formulations are useful for helping you to get alongside your child and working out what might have happened to produce the behaviour that you have just seen. Once you have a better understanding of what has happened and why, you can start to think about what could be changed to make things easier.

It's important to look behind your child's behaviour to see what is really going on.

Principle 5: Keep things calm

Our fifth principle is all about keeping things calm – we know this is often easier said than done.

We know that when children are showing behaviour that adults find difficult, nobody ends up happy. The child is not happy, and is showing this through his behaviour, and the adults are not happy, because they are finding the child's behaviour challenging in some way.

It's important for us to say that children are generally not trying to be challenging, but they are communicating that something is not as they need it to be.

With children with autism, and in fact most children, the behaviour that is challenging you as a parent is only going to get worse if your response is to get cross, angry or upset or to shout.

It's always good to stop and take a breath (and we literally mean take a few slow, deep breaths in and out) or walk into another room for a few moments to gather yourself so you can find a way to be calm when your child is struggling.

We know that this is hard. All parents (including us) can find it hard to present a calm face to their child when he is getting more and more cross, angry or upset. Ask yourself how many times things have not gone well and you have thought to yourself, 'If only I hadn't shouted…'. We've all been there, and part of parenting is learning what didn't go well so you can do it differently next time.

Being calm is a core principle because keeping the emotional temperature low for children with autism, when they are struggling, is so important.

Children with autism often struggle to moderate their own emotional responses, understand the impact of their behaviour on others, understand that someone can be feeling something that they are not and understand the range of emotions in the same way as other children. When you take all of these things together, it makes it all the more important to be the grown up and take on the responsibility for keeping the emotional temperature low.

Principle 6: Be predictable

All children benefit from a predictable environment, and this is also true for children with autism, so this is our sixth principle.

Children generally like to know what is going to be happening to them when, where and with whom. When children are out of their normal routine they can struggle – think about how 'up and down' most children can be during school holidays when many things are different and the normal daily structure is lacking.

Children with autism often have an extra difficulty around predictability because of their overriding desire for things, including people, to be a certain way. This can be seen as a need for sameness, or sometimes as a need for routines, but really it is about the desire for things to be a certain way. We often describe this to parents as a child 'needing it to be the way they need it to be'.

We all like things to be the way we like them, and we can feel unsettled when they are not, even though we're adults. If you put yourself in your child's shoes, you will start to understand that children are generally powerless to change things and often have change thrust on them. Children with autism can find this very difficult to deal with, and when things are not as they need them to be, this can lead to high levels of anxiety.

We talked about anxiety in Chapter 1 and introduced you to the idea of a threshold or limit and the window of tolerance. We want to highlight that where your child is in relation to his threshold or window of tolerance can change day by day or even during a single day.

Principle 7: Think environment

Our seventh principle is thinking about your child's environment.

When a child with autism is struggling, the first thing that adults want to do is to help, and they tend to think that means that the child needs some individual work doing with him. This, after all, is the model that adults use for themselves when they are struggling – they tend to look for individual help or therapy.

Things are, though, not so straightforward for children. Children exist in a world where school and parents are crucially important – after all, children spend most of their waking weekdays at school. This means that they are often having to negotiate two very different settings. Because children don't exist in a vacuum, it is far less straightforward to do something 'to' or with the child in order to make a change. We know that a lot of schools have counselling services that see children on their own (even in primary school) and we don't want to knock these as they are helpful for many children. But we do think that seeing the child as the 'problem' and the person who needs something doing 'to' them is not always going to be helpful. This is especially true for fostered or adopted children.

There are a lot of reasons why you might want to look at the child's environment first.

Our experience tells us time and again that making changes within the child's environment often brings about the biggest change in how the child is managing – it also moves the focus away from the child being the 'problem'.

We need to be clear about what we are talking about when we talk about the environment. We mean how the child experiences his environment and how other people in his environment behave towards him, and also some very practical things about the environment such as noise, smells, temperature and so on.

How your child experiences his environment

How a child with autism experiences his environment is influenced by a whole host of things. Let's remind ourselves of the things that a child with autism *might* find difficult.

You'll remember that we introduced you in Chapter 1 to the main areas of difficulty in autism:

- social communication and social interaction

- rigid and inflexible interests, behaviour and routines

- sensory processing differences

- anxiety.

We have talked in this book about both home and school environments. So, let's take these in turn. We're going to talk about transitions in the next chapter, so you might need to read this section and Chapter 4 to get a really good sense of environmental change.

First, think home environment

Have a think about your home. Are there simple things that you could do to make it a more welcoming place for your child? Have a good look round, or better still ask a trusted friend to, and then think about whether there are any simple environmental changes that are needed.

Here are some examples that focus on sensory processing.

- What is the lighting like?

- Are there particularly smelly rooms or areas that your child may find tricky? Scented candles are just one example of something that you might like but might be too much sensory information for a child with autism.

- Are there appliances in the house that make funny noises that you have got used to but which might startle or frighten a child with autism?

- What do the doorbell and telephone sound like? Are they really loud?

- Are there ways to make it 'just right' for your child?

Think school environment

Children with and without autism spend a lot of their time in school. If your child is moving to a new school when he comes to live with you, you might need to visit the school and think with them about things your child may find difficult. If you already know some things about your child from completing the checklist in the Appendix then this will help.

Examples of what might need thinking about include the dinner hall, cloakroom or other small busy spaces, and any school bells, which can be overwhelmingly loud for children with autism. Transitions are going to be important to think about too – we'll cover these in Chapter 4.

How you understand your child can affect how others behave towards him, because you can use what you know to help other people to understand him. If you have shouty and loud people in your home then you might need them to behave differently, for example, and this is always easier if people understand why.

Let's summarise our seven principles:

- Principle 1: Know your child (and his autism).

- Principle 2: Get alongside your child.

- Principle 3: Understand the communication in your child's behaviour.

- Principle 4: Look behind your child's behaviour.

- Principle 5: Keep things calm.

- Principle 6: Be predictable.

- Principle 7: Think environment.

Key strategies

Now that we've talked about our key principles, we're going to move on to the second part of this chapter, which is about thinking of some of the strategies that might help you to be the best parent you can be to your autistic child.

We've broken this down into lots of specifics because children are all different, as are the families they live in. We hope to include something in here that will chime with you.

There are lots of books about what works well for children with autism – you can find some of our favourites in Chapter 9. Remember we are not going to give you a list of 'how to' strategies because we want to encourage you to understand *your* child, and we hope we have made a start on that with our seven principles.

When you understand your child and have developed an understanding of *why* things are happening, this will help you to see which strategies might work for him.

We're going to give you an understanding of some key strategies that might be helpful and we'll point you in the right direction if you want to learn more about them. We'll also point you in the direction of who else might be a source of expertise and work as a team with you to help your child.

The main strategies we will cover in this section are:

- visual and story aids
- sensory strategies
- communication strategies
- managing anxiety.

We have already talked about keeping things calm and predictable, but we could just as easily have talked about these things here – they are important strategies.

Visual and story aids

One of the simplest ways to get alongside an autistic child is to help him to understand what is going on, and one of the simplest and most effective ways to do this is to use visual or story aids.

Your child's level of overall ability and their language ability will be the best guide to which might work best. You'll remember that we have already said that what works well for children with autism tends to work well for all children, and visual aids are no exception. If you have ever spent time in a really good Foundation or Year 1 class, you will have seen visual aids in the form of visual timetables being used to the benefit of *all* the children.

We are going to talk about visual and story aids together because they serve a very similar purpose.

Visual aids include visual timetables and social scripts in picture form – we'll cover social scripts in picture form when we cover social scripts in the next section.

Visual timetables

These are simple representations in picture form of what is due to happen. They are very easy to make. The ones we're using as examples here have been created on a standard laptop.

Think about your normal morning routine. Many children tend to learn this pretty quickly through repetition because it is generally the same every day. It might take a child with autism longer to learn and the routine in your home might be very different from what a fostered or adopted child is used to. They are going to need a reminder of what they are expected to do. You might think that all morning routines are the same but not everyone gets dressed before breakfast, and some people brush their teeth before breakfast while some brush them after.

Figure 3.4 shows an example of what a visual timetable for the morning routine might look like. It shows getting up, having breakfast, getting dressed, doing hair and teeth, getting in the car and then going to school.

Figure 3.4: Visual timetable for the morning routine

Visual timetables are really useful because they can be easily changed, for example if you are going to be staying at someone else's house or doing something different. They can be used forever or just until your child can manage the routine on his own.

They can be printed out and laminated or cut up and stuck on a strip of Velcro. That way, your child can take off each step as he does it. There are a lot of different ways to use them.

We hope you can see that you can easily make your own – you could even draw them – and they are really adaptable. If your child gets used to using one he should be able to use one for something a bit different, like making transitions at school. We'll cover these in Chapter 4.

Social Stories™ and social scripts
You may have heard people talk about Social Stories™ – this is a method developed by Carol Gray to support the social skills of people with autism. The way they work is to describe a social situation, the social cues, other people's perspectives, etc. and to suggest an appropriate way for the person with

autism to respond to the situation. The aim is for the person with autism to understand what is going on and what the expectations of others in the situation are. They can be used to help an autistic child with things like not talking when someone else is talking, understanding how other people might behave in a certain situation and so on. The aim is to have the information set out in a clear way to help with understanding a complicated situation or one he has struggled with before. One thing they are really good for is helping to reduce a child's anxiety about a situation.

There is a set format for developing Social Stories™ and someone developing something similar cannot call it a Social Story™ unless it fits Carol Gray's criteria.

Many people use the term 'social story' when they are actually talking about a social script or a visual way of helping someone with autism understand a situation.

A social script is a looser way of defining something that can be helpful for a person with autism – they are often comic strips (sometimes called comic strip conversations, also developed by Carol Gray), which is where the name 'script' comes from, but other people use the term more loosely to describe something that is designed to help a child with autism to understand what he 'should' do in a given situation.

We don't want you to get too bogged down in whether you should use a Social Story™, a social script, a script, a comic strip or just a visual way of representing what a desired behaviour from a child with autism in a given situation should look like. The key thing is that you should have some understanding of the difference and not use the name Social Story™ if it is not one. Carol Gray's website has some fabulous examples of Social Stories™ so you can see exactly what they are, along with helpful information about writing a social story (www.carolgraysocialstories.com); The National Autistic Society website (www.autism.org.uk) is also useful.

We really like Social Stories™ when they are used correctly, along the lines that Carol Gray set out, and we would encourage you to use them, but we appreciate that not everyone has the time to do these. We want to encourage you to experiment to find things that work for you and your child.

A social script might use the same kind of visual imagery that a visual timetable would use or it may be something with more words for a child who has good language skills. It may be much more personalised by using photographs – you could use the camera in your mobile phone. We have made a very basic social script, which you can see in Figure 3.5. We hope that you can see that you could easily do this yourself. By using photographs or better drawings you could make it personal to your child.

The key feature is that it should be useful and child centred and tell the child what he needs to do to meet other people's expectations. The one we have shown you in Figure 3.5 is to teach what the child needs to do, but we have also included another social script that uses words rather than pictures.

A WORDY SOCIAL SCRIPT

My name is Jamil and I am in Year 3.

I like to be first in the line for everything and this can get me into trouble with my Teacher.

I can sometimes forget what I am meant to do to get ready to go out at break-time because I really want to get to the door first.

These are the things I need to do:
First I need to wait until my Teacher tells us all that it is break-time.

Then I need to get my coat from my peg.

Then I need to line up with the rest of my class at the door and I need to remember that I need to join the back of the line and not try to be at the front.

When my Teacher is happy that everyone is lining up properly then we can go out for playtime.

At the end of playtime I need to remember to join the back of the line to come back into the classroom and remember not to try to be at the front.

When I come in to the classroom I need to hang up my coat on my own peg and then sit on my place on the carpet.

Figure 3.5: An example visual aid to help a child learn how to meet expectations

Sensory strategies

Sensory strategies are so important for children with autism, because it is much easier for a child to feel safe when their sensory processing is more regulated. The opposite is also true – that it is hard to feel safe when feeling overwhelmed by sensory overload. Remember our window of tolerance from Chapter 1.

There are lots of sensory strategies that can be used for children with autism, but they do need to be based on a good understanding of what is causing a problem for a particular child. When you know your child and know what causes problems for him and when, you are in a much better place to be able to put the right sensory strategies in place. Putting any old sensory strategy in place may work, but it has a much better chance of working when you know whether you need an alerting one or a regulating/calming one.

A child who is feeling overwhelmed in a situation may need a calming strategy whereas a child who is in need of alerting needs an alerting strategy.

We really like *The ASD Feel Better Book* by Joel Shaul, which talks about using strategies to help a child with autism get what he needs when he doesn't feel quite right. The book contains learning strategies that you can photocopy to help with 'feeling better'.

Of course, sensory strategies are not just useful at home, they can also be invaluable at school. At home a child might be able to get up and do some stretching to help with feeling restless, but this probably won't go down too well at school. Unless, that is, the school are part of the 'team' for him and know that he may sometimes need to do some specific and different activities to help him feel 'just right'.

We talked a little about a 'sensory diet' in Chapter 1, and this is a really important concept for all of us – professionals, parents, carers and school – to understand. A sensory diet can help a child with autism to feel 'just right', and this can be enormously important in helping to minimise anxiety.

When autistic children are able to talk about their anxiety, they often talk about this in terms of sensory processing difficulties, so if we can intervene on the sensory processing side (often through managing the environment) then we can reduce anxiety, and reduced anxiety leads to children (and adults) being much more able to cope.

Here are some examples of sensory strategies.

- Being able to stretch, move or go outside when feeling restless.

- Lying down or finding a quiet space away from other people when feeling tense.

- Being able to have firm pressure touch (using something like a weighted blanket) when feeling 'not right'.

- Being able to listen to music when feeling overwhelmed.

- Being able to eat certain sensory foods, such as chewy food.

- Being able to handle sensory toys, such as fidget toys or putty.

We hope you'll see that sensory strategies are not particularly difficult. The key thing is knowing what your child needs and when – and that adults understand this.

We know that children who move around a lot (like many fostered and adopted children) can struggle to feel safe. Sensory strategies are a really good way of creating safety.

If your child is about to move in to live with you, or has recently moved in with you, you can use the checklist in the Appendix to find out what sensory strategies have helped previously, so you can get a head start on the task of creating a safe home environment. For example: if he uses a weighted blanket then you might want to get one; if he listens to music then you might want to make sure that you have headphones he can use; if he needs to move around or do particular exercises as part of his sensory diet then you might want to make sure that there is a space in the house where he can do this without him needing an adult to move furniture.

We hope that you are getting the picture that this is all part of the journey of knowing your child – if you can try to match his sensory needs then you are likely to find this journey all the more rewarding.

Communication strategies

Knowing how your child communicates is, obviously, hugely important, but we appreciate that it can be difficult to know everything about fostered or adopted children before they come to live with you.

Hopefully, you will know if your child uses language or not before he comes to live with you, but language and communication are not the same thing. You will remember from Chapter 1 that autism is a problem with social communication, which includes how your child uses language, the way he looks at you, how he uses gesture, how he uses body language, how close he stands to others, how he understands jokes, sarcasm and metaphors, how he understands the communication (words, body language, intention, etc.) of other people and so on. Communication is a complicated business and having some strategies to help your child communicate is going to be important.

Here are some strategies that might be really helpful.

- Understanding how your child communicates and how he uses language.

- If your child is non-verbal or uses very limited speech, then knowing the communication system he uses is crucial – this might be PECS® or something similar.

- Help your child to process language that he does not understand – this will not always be complex language, it might be helping him to understand language where there is more than one meaning or where someone has made a joke and he has not realised.

- Help your child to understand what others mean when they do or say certain things.

- Be really clear about the link between how someone feels and what they might show on their face, helping your child to understand what other people's faces might be telling him. Help your child to think about the expression that is on his face when he is in certain situations – smiling when being told off at school never goes down well!

- Offer limited choices rather than open-ended questions, so instead of asking, 'What do you want for tea?' you could ask, 'Do you want pasta or fish fingers?' Choice can feel overwhelming to a child with autism and can lead to outbursts over relatively minor things, like what he wants to eat. Another example of where choice can be tricky is getting dressed – if you know what your child likes to wear, you could put out two choices of clothes rather than asking him to, 'Go up and get dressed.'

- Be really clear when you give instructions or use language – try not to use metaphors (things like 'I laughed till I cried' or 'You'll kick yourself when you realise') because they are not easily understood. Anything that has more than one meaning runs the risk of being unclear, even if it is an expression that you think everyone would know.

Anxiety management

Managing your child's anxiety is likely to be much easier if you have got some of these other strategies in place already. This is because a lot of the anxiety that autistic children feel is related to things not feeling right, sensory processing differences and a real fundamental difficulty with understanding other people. Imagine yourself in a room full of people who only speak Japanese. If you don't speak Japanese, then you are likely to find it a very confusing experience. Furthermore, if all those Japanese speakers are trying to get you to do something but you don't understand what it is, things are only likely to feel more confusing.

A child with autism can struggle to put himself in your shoes, but you can try to put yourself in his. Are there things in a given situation that you can see might make him anxious? Are the things that people are suggesting might be helpful actually more likely to make his anxiety worse?

Understanding that your child can feel very anxious is a massive first step here. You might be the only person who sees what your child is going through as being about anxiety. Remember that how an autistic child looks on the outside may not match the emotional state they are feeling on the inside; they may look angry or aggressive but might actually be feeling highly anxious. They might not be able to label it as anxiety, but if you understand that it *might* be anxiety then you can help others to understand that too.

Helping your child to find the right words to label how he is feeling will also help, because, in the long run, it should help him to communicate how he is feeling to others. It is not going to be straightforward though and might take quite a bit of work to get him to be able to tell you how he is feeling, use the right word to describe it and tell others.

EXAMPLES OF USEFUL STRATEGIES
Social Stories™/social scripts
- Social Stories™ need to follow Carol Gray's guidance (www.carolgraysocialstories.com).

- Social scripts use visual imagery and photographs to make them more relevant to your child.

- The aim is to help your child predict what might happen and how he and other people might respond.

- They can work well for managing anxiety, making expectations clear and helping your child to understand how he might behave.

Sensory strategies

- These can have a remarkable effect on your child.

- They should be very simple and straightforward but need to be linked to what is causing him problems.

- They might include things like:

  - being able to stretch, move or go outside when feeling restless

  - lying down or finding a quiet space away from other people when feeling tense

  - being able to have firm pressure touch (using something like a weighted blanket) when feeling 'not right'

  - being able to listen to music when feeling overwhelmed.

Communication strategies

- Knowing how your child communicates and what he finds difficult is the key here.

- They are designed to help your child communicate – to get his needs met and to help others understand him better.

- Help him to process language that he does not understand, including helping him to work out other people's intentions.

- Help him to make the link between how someone feels and what they might show on their face and how he thinks about his own facial expressions.

- Give limited choices to reduce anxiety.

- Be clear in the language that you use and avoid using metaphors or sayings.

Managing anxiety

- Using lots of the strategies in this box will help manage your child's anxiety.

- Understanding that your child might be anxious is crucial and you can then use this understanding to help other adults understand that your child is anxious, even if it might not appear that way at first sight.

- Help your child to work out how he is feeling and help him to find the right words to use to describe that feeling.

Thinking about tricky situations

This section is about managing tricky situations. If you've skipped through to this part, it's going to make more sense if you go back and read the whole of this chapter. This is because you need to be aware of our seven principles to deal with tricky situations and to have some idea about the key strategies we've outlined.

It's also going to be important to think about the things that you know about your child, his autism, threshold and window of tolerance and how you know where he is in relation to those things, and then try to match what is happening to what your child needs.

- If your child needs a low sensory environment, and you know this, then you will need to try to achieve this for him.

- Try to understand why things have worked and why they have not, and try not to throw the baby out with the bathwater.

- Provide simple strategies to help your child to cope – at home, when you are out and in school.

- Help others understand your child, including professionals and the school.

- Get the support that you need – this might need to be at home, with other parents and online.

- Don't give yourself a hard time – nobody gets it right all the time.

We have already talked about what 'behaviour' actually is and how much communication there is in behaviour and we have encouraged you to look behind the behaviour in front of you to try to work out *what* is going on and *why*. We're reminding you of the *what* and *why* in Figure 3.6 – you will have seen a similar diagram in Chapter 2 but we have added 'intervention' into it here. The *what* and the *why* should lead you into thinking about *how* to make a change. Remember that if you just try to deal with behaviour in a general way then you might chance on a good strategy, but you probably won't and, even if you do, you won't know why it is working.

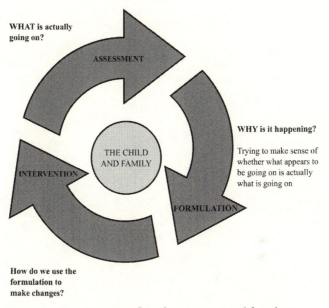

WHAT is actually
going on?

ASSESSMENT

WHY is it happening?

Trying to make sense of
whether what appears to
be going on is actually
what is going on

THE CHILD
AND FAMILY

INTERVENTION

FORMULATION

How do we use the
formulation to
make changes?

Figure 3.6: How intervention flows from assessment and formulation

We want to remind you that thinking about *what* is a problem, *who* it is a problem for and *when* it is a problem are also important.

Remember that some things are acceptable in one situation (for example, at home) but not acceptable in other situations. As an example, it is acceptable to wander round in your pants and a t-shirt all day if you are at home, but much less acceptable to go out and do the weekly food shop dressed this way. It is not wearing pants and a t-shirt that is a problem but rather where it is that you are wearing them.

It is also important to think about all the things that you cannot see that might influence your child's behaviour. We have tried to show in Figure 3.7 how some of these hidden things might have influenced Jamil when he hit Lizzie. This is just an illustration of some of the influences – there will be more!

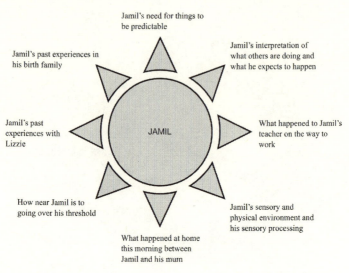

Jamil's need for things to be predictable

Jamil's interpretation of what others are doing and what he expects to happen

Jamil's past experiences in his birth family

Jamil's past experiences with Lizzie

JAMIL

What happened to Jamil's teacher on the way to work

How near Jamil is to going over his threshold

Jamil's sensory and physical environment and his sensory processing

What happened at home this morning between Jamil and his mum

Figure 3.7: Some of the things that could influence Jamil's behaviour

Managing tricky situations

We know that many autistic children will have difficulties with some predictable things, which might include:

- food

- managing on play dates with other children

- sleep

- aggression and behaviour outbursts (tantrums).

We're still not going to give you 'how to' strategies for managing these but instead we want to give you some things to think about. Remember that all autistic children and their circumstances are different, so the reasons underlying their behaviour will also be different.

Here are some pointers though.

Food

This is often an issue and it is generally problematic because of an autistic child's desire for sameness.

- Foods come in lots of different textures and children with autism tend to prefer foods that are predictable in texture – you will know what your child likes. Have a think about whether there are sensory factors at play in terms of texture.

- Autistic children often like food in a certain place on their plate and not touching anything else – they may also only want to eat a restricted range of foods. Having baked beans for tea every day is probably going to be okay!

Our advice around food is to be aware of how your child's autism is impacting on what is problematic and then think about whether changing things will cause unnecessary distress or whether your child's diet is so restrictive so as to be nutrient deficient.

Managing play dates

These are going to be problematic because autistic children have difficulties with social communication and social interaction; they may also struggle to tolerate other people playing with them and struggle to play imaginatively to the same degree as other children.

You know all this already, but if you set things up in the right way then they may just go well. Be prepared to structure the play and be around more than you would perhaps expect to be in order to deal with any difficulties. You know your child and what he is likely to struggle with, so if you try to avoid some of those things then the chances of a successful play date are much higher.

Sleep

Sleep is problematic for lots of fostered and adopted children, not just those with autism. Again, you know your child, and if you learn about his autism you will be able to identify some of the things that are interfering with good sleep – yours as well as his.

Think about what your child might have learned about sleep in his home life before coming to live with you. Did he have a good sleep routine? Perhaps your child needs to learn a healthy routine, and a visual timetable could help with this.

Also consider whether night-time in a previous home was a time when frightening things happened, such as loud arguments between adults. Your child might need you to focus on ensuring that night-times are calm and predictable.

Sensory difficulties might well be at play for children who cannot settle. Consider whether your child needs some particular sensory input to help him. Does he need heavy bedclothes (perhaps a weighted blanket) in order for him to feel 'just right' or a massage? He might or might not. This is why we are not giving you 'how to' strategies because different children will need different things to enable them to feel 'just right'. We want you to be thinking on your child's level and trying to work out what is getting in the way of good sleep.

Aggression and behaviour outbursts

Again, we can't tell you what you should do because we do not know why your child is struggling. Take the time to think about your child and his autism, bearing in mind our seven principles. This will help you to work out why he is struggling.

In autistic children who struggle with outbursts, the problem is almost inevitably to do with how their autism interfaces with the world. Is he anxious? Is he in pain? How would you know? Do you know if he can tell you how he feels, and, if not, how can you help to get behind the difficult behaviour in front of you?

Managing tricky situations is a question of understanding *why* they are difficult for your child and trying to pre-empt the things that you can predict might be difficult, perhaps using some of our seven principles and key strategies.

Not getting it right all the time

Because children are growing and developing all the time, parenting is a constant game of catch-up. Just when you think you understand your child, he grows and develops. His behaviour changes along with his experiences and you can feel as if you are back where you started.

In reality, you will not be right back at the start because you already know a lot about your child: what makes him tick, what things look like when his teacup is overflowing or he has moved out of his window of tolerance and so on. This means that you are still the expert on your child, even if it doesn't feel like that.

If you feel that your child has changed, you could revisit the checklist in the Appendix and do it again to see what new information your child is showing you.

Remember, though, that parenting is a very tough job and one that nobody gets right all the time. You *are* doing a good job, but you will not always recognise that.

Growing with your child

You will grow with your child because you will become more expert, more skilled at noticing when things are not right and more skilled at making quick changes. You will also be learning to advocate for your child to help others with the benefit of your expertise. *You* are the expert here.

When your child enters a new phase in his development then you will adjust too. This doesn't mean that there will not be problems – bumps along the road – but this is how parenting is. You need to recognise when you need support from family and friends and when you need support from services. Don't be afraid to ask for help. Asking for help does not mean you are failing – far from it – it shows that you recognise when more is needed.

We have included some suggestions for looking after yourself in Chapter 8.

Seeking help

Even if you have all the best strategies that you can think of in place, you and your child might still need extra help, and if this is the case then you should not be shy about asking for it.

For sensory processing issues, you might need an Occupational Therapist – one with training in working with children with sensory issues.

For communication and language difficulties, you might need a Speech and Language Therapist, but don't be put off by the fact that your child can talk – we hope you know by now that communication is about far more than spoken words.

For work on behaviour and anxiety, you will probably need a Clinical Psychologist.

You can find out how to contact all of these professionals in Chapter 9.

SUMMING UP

- Remember the seven overriding principles:
  - Know your child (and his autism)
  - Get alongside your child
  - Understand the communication in your child's behaviour
  - Look behind your child's behaviour
  - Keep things calm
  - Be predictable
  - Think environment.

- Explore whether you can use one of our key strategies:
  - visual and story aids
  - sensory strategies
  - communication strategies
  - managing anxiety.
- There are ways to help manage some common tricky situations that can use what you already know about your child, his autism, threshold and window of tolerance.
- Seek help if you need it.

Remember, if you need extra help then ask for it!

Chapter 4

Everyday Transitions at Home and School

Introduction

This chapter is all about helping your child manage transitions, both big and small, and how to communicate to others about why transition is important and what they can do to help.

There are three main parts to this chapter.

- The transitions between different parts of the school day (which we've called small transitions). We've called these small transitions, but they are often not small at all for a child with autism – so we're going to use 'small' in quotes to help us all remember that they may not be small at all.

- Transitions from one school year to the next and transitions between schools such as when a child moves to secondary school. Big transitions also include moving from living in one place, or with one family, to another. We'll talk about transitions between placements in Chapter 5.

- What we as adults can do to support an autistic child who is struggling with transitions.

We can't cover every possible transition here, but we hope to give enough information for you to think about other transitions in the same way.

Small transitions might feel very big to your child.

Throughout this chapter, we're going to keep your child at the centre of everything. As we've said already, keeping your child at the centre of everyone's thinking might seem to be common sense but we know that it very often does not happen.

You will probably find that we have focused more on 'small' transitions but the principles are going to be the same for 'small' and big transitions. We think there is more recognition of why big transitions can be challenging and less awareness of why the 'small', everyday transitions can be challenging.

A NOTE ABOUT SCHOOLS AND AUTISM

We are going to be talking about schools, and we want to recognise that some of them are excellent, some are good, others are pretty good and others really struggle. We don't want to criticise any school as we know from our clinical experience that they can vary hugely in their ability to meet the needs of a child with autism. Our experience is that schools try to do their best but, with the best will in the world, this is not always possible.

It's also true that schools can 'get it right' for one autistic child but can do less well with another child; this comes back to what we have said before about the differences between individual children with autism.

It is also the case that individual Teachers within a school can vary a lot in how well they understand autism and how well they are able to meet the needs of a specific child.

What this means is that even if it is not going well at the moment in your child's school, this could change. Of course, it can go the other way too, but we want to be clear that there can be lots of reasons for this and we don't want any Teachers reading this to feel that we are criticising them – we really are not.

In the UK, Local Authority schools can get help from the Local Authority specialist teams for children with autism, and in some Local Authorities there will be a specialist autism transition team. Not all Local Authorities have this, but they should all have a resource that a school can draw on for advice, whether this is a team, a specialist Teacher, or specialist Teaching Assistant. The point here is that schools don't need to be on their own in thinking about transitions.

Of course, schools outside of the state sector in the UK cannot draw on Local Authority resources, but they can buy in specialist advice from an independent sector professional with expertise in autism. Parents can also buy in this support.

The 'small', everyday transitions

'Small' transitions often seem so small to adults that the impact on a child with autism can be under-appreciated or missed altogether.

One thing we know is that what adults think of as 'small' transitions are often a very big deal indeed for the child concerned. We also know that even when an autistic child is having a very big response to a 'small' transition, it is not always easy for adults to understand what is going on, especially if this 'small' transition happens every day and is one the child sometimes has no difficulty with. Remembering our teacup and window of tolerance here will help. Our first four principles from the last chapter ('Know your child (and his autism)', 'Get alongside your child', 'Understand the communication in your child's behaviour' and 'Look behind your child's behaviour') will also really help you with these 'small' but often very tricky transitions.

At-home transitions

Even before a child gets to school (or nursery), there are a lot of transitions that need to happen in the home environment. Let's talk about just one of them:

The transition from being snuggled in bed to getting up, ready and prepared to leave the house

For a child with autism, there can be a lot of difficulty in this relatively straightforward routine. As adults, we might think that this morning routine, because it is done every day, will become exactly that – a routine – and that it is not a big deal, but it can be. This can be for all the reasons that every other transition can be challenging (i.e. because it is change, because of how full your child's teacup is or where she is in her window of tolerance, etc.) but for a child with autism who has also become anxious about school, this can be a big transition point. You already know that anxiety can be a problem for children with autism.

So why might the morning be a particularly tricky time for a child with autism? Any child can have difficulties with sleeping; some children need much more sleep than others and there are some children who appear not to need much sleep at all. Even for children who need a lot of sleep or those who need the typical amount of sleep, if sleep does not happen at the right time then waking up at the right time becomes difficult.

SLEEP

Children need different amounts of sleep as they grow, and when they reach adolescence the timing of their sleep can change.

We know that many children with autism have unusual sleep patterns and it is this that can cause some of the difficulties with transitions in the morning.

If, for example, your child needs nine hours' sleep and she is asleep at 9 pm and sleeps all the way through, then she will probably wake up at around 6 am. If, on the other hand, she does not get to sleep until 11 pm and needs nine hours' sleep, she won't naturally wake until 8 am. It is then very difficult for her to get up and function well if she has to be up at 7 am for school.

We know that as many as three quarters of children with autism can have problems with sleep. This is worrying because not having enough sleep can lead to problems with learning, feeling sleepy and falling asleep during the day, and behaviour.

Getting up too late can lead to conflict with parents in the mornings, as can getting up too early for everyone else in the family. Having an argument in the morning is not going to be the best thing for keeping calm and making a smooth transition into school. Principle 5, 'Keep things calm', is going to be really important here.

Conflict in general is not going to be helpful for anyone who is about to do something that already makes them anxious – this is true for all of us and even more so for an autistic child. We know that many autistic children can find school a happy and enjoyable place where things are predictable and they are happy. For other children, however, school, and even the thought of it, makes them feel anxious.

School-day transitions

Parents of children who don't struggle with transitions will probably think that children go to school and come home again and everything else in between just flows smoothly. Of course, the parent of a child who struggles with transitions between different activities will know that this is not the case.

There are so many transitions within the school day – here are just a few typical examples for a primary school child.

- Your child leaving you in the playground.

- Coming into the classroom.

- Moving from putting her coat on her peg to sitting to do quiet reading or have carpet time.

- Making the transition from carpet time to the next activity.

- Going out for break-time, which is unstructured, busy, noisy, etc.

- Coming back into class from break-time.

- Going into the lunch hall.

- There are many more transitions until the end of the school day until the final transition, which is leaving school and re-joining you or another adult who has come to collect her.

- For some children who go to an after-school provision such as a club or childminder, there are yet more transitions.

For children in secondary school, the transitions are multiplied. Here are some examples.

- Leaving home to go to school or leaving you if you have dropped them off.

- For children who get a bus to school, there are the transitions on and off the bus and possibly extra transitions in between as new people get on.

- At school, there are transitions every 40 to 60 minutes as they go between lessons, usually changing classrooms and Teachers.

- The change of lessons is often fast and, for any child who is not well organised, this is tricky.

- It is also tricky for any child worried about being late to the next lesson.

- These transitions are often accompanied by a bell and a noisy and crowded stream of people making their way to the next lesson.

- There are all the usual transitions into and out of break-time and lunch, but these can be more problematic for teenagers with autism because there is a lot less structure and there may be fewer adults around.

- There may also be an expectation that your child will take bags and equipment to and from her locker.

We know that each of these transitions brings challenges for children with autism. Let's look at a couple of them to unpick what might be happening and why it might be difficult for a child with autism.

Separating in the morning

Most children look like they make the transition from their parent or carer into school each morning without a problem. Look a little closer in the playground, though, and you will see quite a few children struggling. Some children might be needing extra hugs, some might be needing their grown up to hand them over to the Teacher (sometimes literally getting the Teacher to make physical contact by holding a hand to indicate the time to go in), some will be tearful and others might be late to school so that they don't have to make this separation in full view of everyone or when the playground is too busy.

Children of all ages can struggle to leave their parent in the morning and this can be for lots of reasons – a child who is feeling poorly, tired or hungry, a child who has fallen out with friends, etc. The point we want to make here is that separating from your parent to go into school is hard for lots of children, but for an autistic child it is the transition from the known and the comfortable to the unknown that can be difficult – even if she has been in that class with that Teacher for a while, it can still feel unknown. It can also feel overwhelming to be surrounded by so many children and adults when all you want to do is stay at home. Don't forget that someone who has sensory difficulties, and who struggles with social chat with others, can find this unstructured busy time very stressful indeed; it is no wonder that it can feel overwhelming.

Going out for break-time

Going out for break-time is normally something that children look forward to – time to run around, chat or play with friends, let off steam and get fresh air. For an autistic child, however, it can be another of those times when things are confusing.

- Rules are unclear or different from the classroom – rough and tumble play may be happening but navigating it is complicated.

- There is not the structure of a lesson.

- It is busy.

- She can feel alone if nobody wants to play with her.

- She may struggle to navigate the complex social world of being with lots of children with very few adults around to structure what is going on.

To add to the difficulty, the child has to stop suddenly at the end of the break-time and may not get any warning of this until the whistle blows. She then has to stop being energetic and be calm, stand still, line up and then go back into another different set of demands in the classroom.

On the positive side, break-time can provide the opportunity for a much-needed movement break. We know that this can be calming and can help some children to regulate sensory and emotional demands.

Going for lunch

As with going out for break-time, lunchtime is often a time that most children look forward to. They eat their lunch, chat to friends, clear up and go out to play. For children with autism, however, lunchtime can be overwhelming.

- It is another unstructured time, so has all the same issues of unstructured activity, such as there being fewer adults around and there being a demand for social interaction.

- Many children with autism eat a restricted diet and may not have the food they want to eat.

- School dinner halls are extremely busy, with people moving around unpredictably, and are very noisy places, which can create sensory overload.

- If they have school dinners then they need to choose their food, carry their tray, find somewhere to sit, etc.

- This is made worse by the smell of the food, and we need to remember that children with autism can be very sensitive to smells and can find them aversive.

Going home at the end of the day

We are not saying that all children with autism will find all of these transition points difficult, but many will struggle with some of them. Many of the parents and children with autism that we have worked with over the years have found the end of the day very difficult and have often struggled to understand why, especially as they have felt that it should be something that an autistic child would look forward to.

There are a few reasons why children with autism might find the end of the school day tricky.

- The change from the structured school setting (which many children with autism find reassuring) to the lack of structure involved in going home may cause anxiety.

- The crush of bodies in the cloakroom at the very end of the day can cause a child with autism to feel overwhelmed by sensory demands.

- For some children, going home provides a release from all the things they have been keeping a lid on all day and their difficulties with emotional regulation mean that this spills over into difficulties with behaviour at the very point when they return to their parent.

Having a Teacher and a school that understands why these 'small' transitions are difficult is going to be crucial in helping your child to manage throughout the day. We don't want any parent to think that their autistic child is having a dreadful time at school day after day – it is unlikely that this is the case – but there will be things that cause anxiety for her around transitions. The understanding that you and the important adults around your child can give her is key.

We've talked before about assessment (*what* is actually going on), formulation (what it might mean: the *why*), intervention (what to do about it) and looking behind the behaviour that is right in front of you. This is so important when thinking about what might be going on for a child with autism when she is struggling with behaviour in school. In our experience, the most common problem is anxiety that is related to a transition (including the anxiety that comes from sensory difficulties). This is the area where really small changes can make such a positive difference. The challenge, though, is recognising what is going on and when, i.e. which transition is causing the distress.

It can be helpful to ask the following questions to try to narrow it down.

- When in the school day do problems tend to happen?

- Is your child generally more unsettled than people would expect when coming back into class after a break?

Are there simple things that can be done to make a big difference? Remember that we have already talked about how environmental changes can make a huge positive difference and how understanding *what* is difficult, *why* and *when* can often suggest straightforward changes.

We'll talk about practical strategies further on, but, in our experience, it can be very small changes that make a very big difference. The key is understanding why they are needed, and this comes from adults looking behind what is right in front of them.

Transitions between schools

We're now going to focus on school transitions.

We recognise that for any child, moving from primary to secondary school is something that can provoke a lot of anxiety, even if everyone else from the same school is moving up with her. Within this context, it is no surprise that moving between schools is a significant transition for a child with autism, but there is also much more involved.

Here are just some of the things that change for any child making the transition to 'big' (i.e. secondary) school.

- Moving from having one Teacher to having as many as ten.

- Having to negotiate all these different Teachers across the week, often with very little contact with most of them.

- Having lessons in different rooms across the day and sometimes in different buildings.

- An unfamiliar layout that can take a very long time to learn.

- Limited time to move between lessons.

- Having to negotiate school corridors, which are rarely big enough for the numbers of children using them.

- Being with new children whom she does not know and has never met.

- Having to wear a more formal uniform, such as stiff shirts rather than polo shirts, a set kind of school shoe, having a set PE uniform, etc. This can lead to multiple difficulties with labels, sleeves and so on.

These differences may be significant for any child, but for an autistic child they come with the added challenge of difficulties with social communication and social interaction, sensory processing differences, rigid and inflexible thoughts, behaviour and routines, and anxiety. It is, therefore, no surprise that this transition is a big one. Often adults will recognise this and put in place a plan for an 'enhanced transition', but because we know that not all children will have a diagnosis of autism by this point in their lives, it is often not until they struggle with making the transition that people realise there is a problem. We'll talk about planning for transitions a little later in this chapter.

There are also positives about moving to secondary school. These include a school with a bigger group of children with autism, more expertise, a dedicated space to go to at unstructured times and often a greater understanding of the breadth of different ways that a child with autism can present.

We also know that, for fostered and adopted children, moving school can be something that happens a lot because they have also been moving between different homes. Moves between schools can provoke a lot of anxiety, especially because these can remind children of other difficult moves they have experienced, for example, their move into foster care.

Transition planning

Let's have a think about how to plan for transitions.

For big transitions, such as moving between schools, school years or placements, making a good transition plan well ahead of time can be the key to making a successful transition.

The aim is to make a good plan with a clear aim and hope that it is not needed, rather than not to make a plan and hope that things will be okay, only to find that they are not. The key principles from Chapter 3 that are going to be important to hold in mind here are Principle 6, 'Be predictable', and Principle 7, 'Think environment'. The key is to prepare your child and be one step ahead of her in thinking about what she might need, so Principle 1, 'Knowing your child (and his autism)', is also going to be needed.

We come across many types of transition plan and they don't have to be big or formal. What they do require, though, is a lot of thought and, crucially, a lot of planning and preparation.

In our experience, transition plans should aim to do all of these things.

- Have the child's needs at the centre (this is Principle 1, 'Know your child (and his autism)').

  - It is no good making a transition plan without considering your child's needs, because it is your child who needs the transition plan, not the adults around her.

  - Having a child-centred plan means involving your child in the transition planning process.

  - It means finding out what your child thinks may be different in the new setting, what information *she* wants to know (which might include photographs, maps, etc.) and what visits she feels *she* wants to make.

  - It can be helpful to have a transition box or folder where your child can keep all the key information that *she* wants.

- Aim to deal with the medium and longer term, not just the first few days or weeks.

- Base the plan on an understanding of what has worked and what has not worked when your child has made transitions in the past (this involves Principle 1, 'Know your child (and his autism)').

- Have a clear aim, such as to reduce anxiety (this involves Principle 3, 'Understand the communication in your child's behaviour', and Principle 6, 'Be predictable'). Having a plan that has to 'ensure a good transition' as its aim is probably not going to work too well because it is not specific enough.

- If your child has physical or significant sensory difficulties then the plan needs to consider these too; this involves you knowing your child's autism well, which is Principle 1.

- If this is a school transition plan, the plan should include practical issues. It might help to try to imagine the things that might make you anxious if someone put you in a brand-new situation; this involves considering Principle 7, 'Think environment', and might include:

  - what the structure of the school day will be like

  - what a possible timetable looks like

  - where the lunch hall is and what the process for getting lunch is

  - where break-time happens and what there is to do

  - what there is to do at unstructured times

  - whom to see and where to go if they have any problems.

A transition plan might include:

- a student 'passport' of some kind – this is generally one side of paper to help school staff to understand your child's strengths and needs, what she likes and does not like, what helps her and what does not help. It should ideally be written with your child, with your help

- a folder or box of key information (or a poster – the idea is that all the information should be in one place) that might include a map of the school, including who is in what office, social space, form rooms, etc., a 'who's who' of staff, an example of a timetable that shows when break-times are, an example of a school planner and so on.

This might sound like a lot of work, but really it is about putting yourself in your child's shoes, trying to understand what might be tricky and making sure that you have covered all these tricky things.

What else can we do to help with transitions, both big and 'small'?

As well as making sure that transition planning happens, the most effective things that adults can do to support a child with autism are to:

- understand that transitions can be difficult

- understand why this might be the case and why transitions might cause difficulties

- recognise when your child is showing, by her behaviour, that she is struggling with a transition

- do something to help.

Let's take these one by one:

Understanding that transitions can be difficult

Reminding ourselves of some of the core things that autistic children can struggle with might help us to understand why transitions can cause challenges. Principle 1, 'Know your child (and his autism)', and Principle 3, 'Understand the communication in your child's behaviour', are going to help here.

Remember that your child may have difficulties with:

- a strong desire or need for sameness – this may mean that she has to do certain things at certain times and in a certain way

- high levels of anxiety

- sensory processing

- communicating her emotions

- understanding the link between her environment and her behaviour (including the impact of others on her and how they are feeling)

- generalising from one situation to another.

Understanding why this might be the case

Let's use some examples to think about why these things might cause a problem with transitions.

We know that many children with autism can struggle with sensory processing and that they can feel overwhelmed.

For many children, the smell of their school dinner wafting through the school in the late morning can be experienced as comforting (because they know hot food is coming and they might be hungry) or exciting (because they know that lunchtime means playtime and even if they are not excited by lunch, they may be excited by going out to play or going to a lunchtime club). For a child with autism, however, the smell of lunch seeping into the classroom can be experienced in any number of ways including:

- making her feel sick because the smell is overpowering

- making her feel anxious because lunchtime equals playtime, which has no rules and where she has nobody to play with.

This can lead to a rising level of anxiety and them moving outside of their window of tolerance, and it is this rising level of anxiety that leads to a child with autism struggling with the transition.

We need to remember that children with autism have a strong need for things to be a certain way and a strong need for sameness, and the constant changes throughout the school day can leave them feeling deeply unsettled over a long period of time.

One way to think about why this feeling of being unsettled can cause problems is to think back to our teapot and teacup – the concept of a threshold. We all know that there can be times when we are upset by something that we would normally cope well with, and this is generally because this small thing is the last in a series of things that have happened and that have overstepped our limit.

Understanding what behaviour might indicate a child is struggling

It is not always easy for adults to work out what a child is trying to communicate. All children communicate through their behaviour, including those who speak very well, but adults are generally not good at listening to this behaviour. Remember Principle 3, 'Understand the communication in your child's behaviour'.

Understanding that transitions might be difficult, and why, and having a good understanding of the fact that a child with autism may find the same transitions difficult day after day, even though they do them every day and they sometimes manage, can make it easier to understand your child's behaviour.

Examples of behaviour that might indicate that a child is struggling with transitions include:

- not being able to come straight in to the classroom and sit on the carpet, despite this being what is expected every day

- needing to be given the same instruction every day, despite it always being the same

- pushing in to the front of the line when going out for break-time, despite being told repeatedly not to.

A child who feels worried or upset when it gets near to break-time might show this by not listening, interfering in other children's personal space, being restless and so on. Older children might show the same feelings by being restless, struggling to comply with adults' requests and so on.

Remember that it is highly unlikely that a child will spontaneously say what is wrong (even if you ask her). Children very often do not know what the matter is, but they do know that things don't feel right. This is why knowing your child (and his autism) (Principle 1) and understanding the communication in your child's behaviour (Principle 3) are so important.

Doing something to help

What, then, can you and other adults do to help? This is a difficult question because it will depend on what it is that is making transitions difficult. We have already talked about the importance of understanding that transitions can be difficult, understanding why that might be the case and why transitions might cause difficulties, and recognising when a child is showing us, by her behaviour, that she is struggling with a transition.

It can be helpful to try to work out whether there are specific transitions that are causing a problem and then trying to understand what it is about those transitions that is causing the problem for the child. For example, it might be that the child is anxious because she is unsure of what is required of them when she enters the new space or activity, or there may be sensory processing needs that are unmet when transitioning from one activity to another.

Practical strategies

Once the *why* of the behaviour is clearer, there may be simple strategies that will help, and we're going to talk about these using some of our core principles.

Knowing your child (and his autism) (Principle 1) is all about understanding what is difficult for your child, and if you put this together with understanding the communication in your child's behaviour (Principle 3) and looking behind your child's behaviour (Principle 4) you will have some powerful ways to make things different. You will have a good understanding of what situations might be tricky and what things might need to be put in place to support your child.

Here's how this might work.

- If the problem is at the start of the day and your child struggles to make the transition into school, support her by providing an adult or activity to bridge the gap or with an arrangement for her to come in to school in the morning a few minutes after everyone else to avoid the morning lining up and cloakroom crushes. This is really about making it predictable for your child (Principle 6) based on the understanding that this is what your child needs and that she finds this transition tricky.

- If the problem is about coming back into a busy cloakroom, try allowing her to come in first when things are quieter or let her get her things before others at the end of the day to avoid the cloakroom crush. Again, this is about knowing your child (and his autism) (Principle 1), thinking environment (Principle 7) and making things more predictable for your child (Principle 6).

- If the social demands of lining up are part of the difficulty, being able to line up first (or last) to avoid the crush of people may help. This involves understanding what your child's pushing and shoving at lining up time is based on and requires an understanding of Principle 3, 'Understand the communication in your child's behaviour', and Principle 4, 'Look behind your child's behaviour'.

- If the problem is with coming in from a busy break-time to sit down to quiet work, support your child to make that transition by providing some kind of bridging activity with an adult or another child. This is similar to the problem of coming in at the start of the day and involves making it predictable for your child (Principle 6) based on the understanding that this is what your child needs and that she finds this transition tricky.

- If the problem is the sensory overload of the lunch hall, make an arrangement for your child to eat her lunch in a place other than the dining hall – this might be with another child for company or she might be allowed to get an early lunch to avoid the busy dinner hall. Again, this is based on knowing your child (and his autism) (Principle 1) and creating a calm environment (Principle 5), which in this case is a low sensory environment.

The possible solutions really are quite endless because the thing that really matters is your attempt to get behind the behaviour that your child has shown. There is no one-size-fits-all solution, but understanding that there is a problem and understanding something about what is causing it is the route to finding a good strategy.

We have already talked in Chapter 3 about social scripts and Social Stories™. These are really good ways of helping your autistic child understand the 'small' transitions from home to school and helping her to understand that the sequence is always the same. This is about trying to create more predictability for your child (Principle 6).

When we use a visual timetable to support transitions, this is also about trying to make things more predictable for your child. Just like the home-to-school transitions that might be supported by a visual timetable, the 'small' transitions at school can be helped by a visual timetable too. Figure 4.1 is an example of how a visual timetable might be used to illustrate the transitions throughout the school day. This could be split into morning and afternoon, but it could really be used in whichever way is helpful.

Morning:

Afternoon:

Figure 4.1: Examples of visual timetables for school

Autistic children can and do manage transitions, even big ones, if the adults around them have thought about what things need to be in place.

SUMMING UP

- Transitions come in all sizes, and what adults think might be small transitions might be a very big deal for your child.

- Transitions start from getting out of bed and go all through the school day.

- Going home can be a tricky transition for a child with autism.

- Transitions can be tricky for lots of reasons – all the reasons that a child with autism might struggle with anything:

  - sensory processing

  - a need for sameness

  - the demands of social communication and social interaction

  - anxiety.

- Adults can support transitions by:

  - understanding that there is a problem related to transitions

  - understanding why that might be the case

  - recognising when a child is showing us that she is struggling with a transition.

- Planning for bigger transitions is crucial – make a good plan that has a clear aim.

Chapter 5

Placement Transitions and Contact

In this chapter, we're going to explore some areas that are important when your child is fostered and adopted. These are:

- transitions that happen between placements

- how to support your child with contact – his visits and communication with his birth family

- how to support your child with involvement from social care professionals.

We're aware that you may already know a bit or a lot about these areas, especially if you're an experienced foster carer or adopter. What we want to do is explore these areas while thinking about what might work well when your child has autism. We'll keep our seven principles from Chapter 3 in mind.

Placement transitions

You may be reading this book in preparation for a child with autism coming to live with you. Perhaps you are an adopter who is about to begin a period of introductions to your child after having your 'match' approved by an Adoption Panel. Or maybe your child is moving to live with you for long-term fostering after being with a short-term carer. Or your child may be moving from living with his birth family to living with you as his foster parent.

We're aware that some children can move into foster care quickly, especially when they have been at risk of harm. At other times, moves between placements will be planned and happen gradually. We're going to look first at moves that are more planned and then look at what can help following a quick move.

What usually happens when a child moves placement?

It's Social Workers who usually identify placements and plan moves. 'Introductions' is the name usually used for the time period during which you and your child meet each other, often for the first time, and begin getting to know each other. Introductions can vary in how long they take – from a few days to weeks. A plan for introductions is usually made by getting key people together; this will include Social Workers, your child's current parents and you, his future parent. Plans for the introduction period are made with the aim of making this major transition in your child's life work well for him and everyone, including you, who is involved.

As part of the planning process for introductions, Social Workers will gather lots of information about your child so that you get to know some of the important things about him *before* he moves to live with you. Hopefully, you will also have the chance to ask your child's current parent for information. You may meet other adults who know and support your child, such as School Teachers and health professionals.

In addition to the usual information that is collected and shared with you, it's helpful to gather some specific information about how your child does things, such as social communication and social interaction, i.e. 'the autism-bit', so that you can prepare yourself and your home for him. This is all part of Principle 1, 'Know your child (and his autism)'. We think that the more information you have, the better prepared you can be for a smoother start for life with your child.

What is useful to know when preparing for your child to come to live with you?

If you're at the pre-introductions part of getting to know your child, you are going to have to rely on getting information from other people. You haven't yet had the experience of being with your child. To help you to gather useful information, remember that we've put together the Appendix, which covers the main areas. You can ask his current parents and other people who know him well to complete it.

You can also use the Appendix to develop your understanding of your child as you get to know him during introductions and beyond. Your knowledge of your child is obviously going to grow and develop over time. Our intention is that the Appendix can be used to guide your understanding of your child, rather than it being something you need to get right and complete. Your understanding of your child will actually never be complete because he is never going to be finished. He will grow and change throughout his childhood.

How can you assist your child's future parents?

If you're currently parenting a child who you know is going to move to another placement, perhaps because you are a short-term carer, then it'll be really helpful for you to gather information about his autism for his future parents. You could be saving everyone, especially your child, a lot of trial and error in the future by sharing what you know helps him to communicate and feel comfortable ('just right') at home and school. Don't assume that things you know about your child will be obvious to other people or that others will provide the information – you know your child best.

Good preparation for a change in placements begins with knowing about your child's autism.

Preparing for introductions

The introductions period and moving in time can be very intense and tiring for everyone, especially your child. Moving to a new home is stressful for children and involves more loss and change. It's a massive transition. Your child with autism could find adapting to change really stressful because he is likely to be more comfortable when life is predictable and contains sameness. For your child, meeting you as his new parent will bring along a whole new influx of sensory experiences and interactions. It can be very overwhelming.

Most fostering and adoption services have their usual ways of planning and supporting introductions. They'll be aiming to make the process as comfortable as possible for your child and you. It's worth checking that some autism-friendly strategies are used.

What can help before face-to-face introductions begin?

There are lots of things that can help with the transitions *before* you and your child meet face to face properly for the first time. We'll organise these ideas by looking at how to make an autism-friendly plan for the move and then move on to how to prepare your child, yourself and your home.

Make an autism-friendly plan for the move

When planning for introductions, it's really useful to prepare for as much of the autism-stuff that you can. We can both recall times when we haven't prepared for things as well as we thought we had and then things went astray and we wished we'd planned more. It's quite hard to plan too much! When your child has autism, it's even more useful to have a comprehensive plan, even if you then don't need to do everything that you prepared for. Plans can help everyone involved to feel less anxious during the transition. So, bearing in mind Principle 6, 'Be predictable', use the following points to help you prepare.

- Plan the introductions so that your child has a routine to follow and does not have to move between too many activities. Try to keep new experiences to a minimum. Meeting you will be enough of a new experience for him.

- Make sure that everyone knows the plan so that it is predictable and doesn't change more than it needs to.

- Think about whether a visual aid or social script, like the ones we talked about in Chapter 3, might be helpful so your child knows what is happening.

Watch out for assumptions about how introductions should be done

As we said earlier, many fostering and adoption social work departments will have their own way of doing introductions. However, when your child has autism, you can't assume that you can follow the usual process. For example, Social Workers will typically get you to build up the time you spend with your child and have as much contact with your child as possible. This is for two reasons. First, it's really helpful to know your child's daily routines, such as what time he goes to bed, because maintaining the same routines can lessen the trauma of the move. Second, Social Workers will want you to have lots of direct hands-on experience of doing key tasks with your child, such as his bedtime routine. This is advice that is well intentioned and aimed at ensuring that you have practical knowledge of parenting your child. However, this advice might not work when your child has autism. For example, bedtimes could become very stressful if his routine changes too much and involves a new adult.

So be led by your child and his autism. For example, if your child is going to become distressed and anxious if you do a particular part of his routine then don't do it. There are other ways in which you can find out what his routine is like and how to follow the routine together. You don't need to have physically done every routine or task with your child before he comes to live with you, especially if it will cause unnecessary anxiety for him. Introductions and meeting new people is already stressful enough for your child.

Ideas to help prepare your child before introductions

Your child's current parent and Social Worker are going to be the main people who will prepare him for the move. Before you begin introductions (as his future parent), you can help your child's current parents by:

- providing your child with pictures of you and your home. This is something that most adopters are encouraged to do. You might have been asked already to create a book that contains pictures of you and your home for your child.

The following tips will make introductory picture books more autism-friendly.

- Label the pictures, even if the picture seems obvious. For example, label the picture of your bedroom, your child's bedroom, the kitchen, etc.

- Begin your book with a picture of the outside of your house and then have a page with a picture of each room, starting with the entrance hall of your house. Clear sequences like this work well.

- Take a picture of each room from the doorway, so your child will see what he will see when he first enters the room.

- Take a picture of the main feature of each room, for example, a picture of his bed in his bedroom and label it.

- Include pictures of you, other people and any pets that live in your house. Label each person and what their role is.

- Resist the temptation to decorate each page too much. Some children with autism can get easily distracted if there is too much stimulation on each page. For example, if your child has a particular fixed interest in sparkly or bright things then he may focus only on the sparkly stickers on the page and not anything else.

- Make sure that you do not change the appearance of your home after you have sent the picture book to your child. Your child may become fixated on what your home looks like and will then get confused if it looks different when he actually visits it. He could get confused if the lounge walls have been painted a different colour. It can be really important to keep things the same as they were in the pictures.

- You could include a page that shows what a regular day looks like. This is where a simple visual timetable can help. Remember that a visual timetable is something that can be used with your child for a short time to help him understand a new situation. Having a visual timetable that sets out what a typical day in your house is like does not mean that you will have to follow that routine forever; it's just a tool to help your child understand that his new home will have order and predictability. This is Principle 6, 'Be predictable'.

- Think carefully about the language you use. For example, your child may have no concept of what a 'forever mummy' means. This is just the sort of thing that a Social Story™ is designed to deal with. So, decide with the Social Worker and child's current Social Worker how a forever mummy will be explained to your child. Write the script for what a forever mummy is. The key thing is for everyone to use the same words when explaining things. Figure 5.1 shows what a social script for a forever mummy *could* look like for Jamil – our made-up child who is moving to adoption.

- Use of the words 'new mum' or 'new dad' may raise anxiety – your child will need to know what these words mean.

You could also do the following.

- Make a video of yourself and your home for your child. To make videos more autism-friendly, it's helpful to:

  - use simple and clear language when you speak; try not to speak too much – a simple, 'Hello I am Jenny' is fine

  - keep it short – two minutes maximum

  - move the camera slowly and focus on one thing at a time; do not use fast action shots

  - avoid adding background music.

Figure 5.1: A social script to explain a forever mummy

Ideas to help your child before he moves – if you are his current parent

- Look through the picture books that have been prepared by his future parent – choose moments during the day when he is calm and settled.

- Use the same words that everyone else is using to explain things to your child. For example, terms such as 'forever mummy'.

- Keep explanations about the move simple and straightforward. Think about whether you can use a social script or a visual timetable to explain what is happening.

- If he asks the same questions about what's going to happen then that's okay. Just keep giving the same information in a simple way. A lot of autistic children ask the same questions over and over again (it can be part of the rigid and inflexible interests, behaviour and routines aspect of autism). Asking repeated questions does not necessarily mean that he does not know the answer – it might just be reassuring for him to hear the same answer, even if it can feel a bit irritating to you.

- Tell your child that you will tell his future parent everything they need to know to help him feel 'just right'.

- Check if your child has any questions about his future parent.

- Your child may react to being told about his move by becoming anxious about which of his daily routines will be disrupted. This may cause more anxiety than the impact of losing you as his current parent.

- Prior to the move, maintain his home and school routines and avoid any changes – even small ones.

Helping your child with the end of his placement with you

Placement transitions are about beginnings and endings. Your child will be experiencing the loss of you, your home and other people and places. As his current parent, here are some things to think about.

- Does your child understand why this ending is happening? Will a social script help explain the move?

- How can your child say goodbye?

- Would a goodbye party suit your child? Could this happen in a low-key and calm way?

- Could you take photos of your child, you and other people he is saying goodbye to? You could organise these pictures in a book (with clear labels of who everyone is). He can then look at them once he has moved.

- Can you create a goodbye letter, card or picture for your child to keep?

Ideas to help you, as his future parent, get prepared before introductions

The best preparation begins with you getting the information you need from your child's current parent.

- Ask your child's current parent what your child will want to know about you.

- Ask your child's parent to share information about your child's autism and sensory needs. This is you making a start on Principle 1, 'Know your child (and his autism)'. You can use the Appendix to do this.

- It may be very difficult to know how your child is making sense of and coping with introductions. Your child's emotional expressions may be hard to 'read'. Always ask your child's current parent what they have learned about how he shows he is settled or distressed. This will help you to gauge whether your child is feeling 'just right' or is overwhelmed or anxious during introductions. This is you making a start on Principle 3, 'Understand the communication in your child's behaviour', and Principle 4, 'Look behind your child's behaviour'.

- Ask your child's current parent what helps him feel better when he is anxious so that you have an idea of what you can do. Don't be surprised though if the strategies used by his current parent don't work so well for you. It's not a reflection on your ability. Be patient with yourself and him. Accept that your child is going through a major change, so the usual strategies may not work so well while you're first getting to know him.

- Manage your own expectations. You may be feeling very excited, and nervous, about meeting your child, and you may have many ideas about how you want to spend time with him. Your child, on the other hand, probably has his own preferred activities, some of which may seem unusual! He may enjoy doing mundane activities such as lining up objects, gazing at shiny objects or watching the same DVD repeatedly. This is your child putting Principle 6, 'Be predictable', into action for himself!

Ideas to help you prepare your home

- Try to predict what might be difficult for your child, and make changes in advance, for example, declutter your lounge if you need to! Organise your home so that objects and things are in a logical place. It can really help to have a place for everything in your home, for example keeping shoes in the same place. When your child moves in, this will help him and you to feel organised. This is Principle 7, 'Think environment'.

- Imagine that you are your child to help you try to predict what it'll be like for him to be in your home. Take a slow walk around your home 'as if' you are your child. What can you see? What can you hear? What can you feel? What can you smell? What will it be like for him? What will make your home be 'just right' for him?

- Put labels on your room doors, such as 'toilet', 'kitchen'.

- Check whether your child's current parent is using visual aids within the home. For example, check whether there is a visual aid in the bathroom, which shows him the sequence involved when using the toilet. If visual aids are being used currently then get copies of these so they are ready for him in your home.

What can help during face-to-face introductions?
Ideas to help your child

- Use a visual timetable so your child knows what is happening. You can use symbols on cards with Velcro on the back that you can move around on a Velcro strip. It can sometimes be helpful to have two timetables: one that has a very simple overview of the week and another that focuses upon what will happen that day or during the next couple of hours. Be guided by what your child needs to help him feel organised. Some children can struggle with the concept of time so having too many activities shown can feel overwhelming and confusing. Principle 1, 'Know your child (and his autism)', is what you are developing here.

- Be mindful of how your child shows how he is coping. Don't assume that your child's emotional expression reflects how he is feeling underneath; a child with autism may have a mismatch between how he appears to you and how he is actually feeling inside. Remember also that your child may not be able to label his emotions. This is our Principle 3, 'Understand the communication in your child's behaviour'.

- Think about your approach – remember your child may feel completely overwhelmed even if you can't tell. Be quiet, calm and slow in movement when you first meet him. This is our Principle 5, 'Keeping things calm'.

- Join him in his play. You can put Principle 2, 'Get alongside your child', into place here by playing alongside him as we described in Chapter 3.

- Give him time to respond to you. Remember that it might take him longer to process what's going on around him. He might find it difficult to process different types of information at the same time (simultaneous processing). For example, if you are talking to him when there is also a television or music on, he might find it difficult to cope with these two types of sensory inputs at the same time.

- Think carefully about your use of physical touch. Your child may be very sensitive to touch, so it's important to find out how he responds to touch by asking his current parent. It's also important to know how he does physical touch and how you should respond to this. For example, some children explore new people by touching them, getting too close or smelling them. Find out how his current parent responds to this so that you can be consistent. This is another example of how you are learning about him and his autism – Principle 1.

- Be aware that your child may show an increased intensity in his special interest or he may develop more detailed rituals or repetitive behaviours. These are his way of coping with the anxiety from the change in his life.

Ideas to help you, as his new parent, during introductions

- Manage your own emotional expression. Don't be too big with your emotions. Don't keep looking at your child, especially when you meet him for the first time. It can be really hard not to look intently at your child when you are meeting him face to face for the first time, but try not to stare – he may find this uncomfortable. Remember that once he is at home, you will have lots of time to look at him. You'll soon be able to experience the pleasure many parents feel when they are able to watch their child intently when they are peacefully asleep.

- Figure out what will help you to feel as calm as possible during this big change in your life.

What can help once your child has moved into your home?
Ideas to help your child

- A visual timetable can be used to give your child a plan of what happens in your house during a typical week; you may need to do different timetables for different rooms (for example, one upstairs that shows the 'morning' routine, one downstairs that shows the 'going to school' routine, etc.) It's time to invest in some strips of Velcro and a laminator!

- Develop routines from the start – this is Principle 6, 'Be predictable'.

- Give your child a special place to sit at mealtimes and sit together while watching television. It can be helpful if you can let your child choose his special place. This is also Principle 6, 'Be predictable'.

- For older children, it can be helpful to provide simple explanations about what to expect and what the 'rules' may be in your home. Try to keep this literal and concrete.

- Try not to offer too many choices to your child. Open-ended questions where the choices are endless could make him feel anxious, so rather than asking, 'What do you want for tea?', you could ask if he wants pasta or fish (or any other food). The point is to offer a limited selection for him to choose from.

Remember that the strategies and core principles from Chapter 3 will also be helpful.

How to help your child when he has moved in an emergency or unplanned way

If your child has moved to live with you in a quick and unplanned way, your focus will be upon wanting to help him settle and ensuring that he understands what has happened. Here are some ideas for helping him.

Using Principle 1, 'Know your child (and his autism)', try to gather as much information as you can about him using the checklist in the Appendix. Talk to your child's previous parents (if possible), Social Workers, Teachers and other people who know him. You want to gather as much knowledge as you can so that you can reorganise your home and your approach with him in a way that best meets his needs.

Using Principle 7, 'Think environment', focus on your home environment. Think about what your child may need in your home to make it feel okay.

When your child has just arrived in your home, he does not know you, your home or your expectations. Helping your child to know what to expect from you and your home will lessen his anxiety. Visual timetables are really helpful. You could have a visual timetable for each daily routine, especially mornings and bedtimes, so that he knows what's going to happen and what's expected of him. Figure 5.2 shows an example of a visual timetable for getting ready in the morning. It shows the sequence of getting out of bed, having breakfast, getting dressed, brushing teeth and hair, driving and going to school.

Figure 5.2: A visual timetable for the morning

Consider what routines your child needs during his day. Remember that how your home is organised and set up is a crucial step towards helping him to feel 'just right' rather than anxious. This is using Principle 6, 'Be predictable'.

Using Principle 3, 'Understand the communication in your child's behaviour', think about what your child might understand about his move. This can be a tricky area because:

- your child may be too young or may struggle to talk so he can't tell you why he has moved

- your child may struggle to answer questions such as, 'Do you know why you have moved here?' or 'What happened?'

It can help to take a very matter-of-fact approach that involves you giving him a very simple explanation of what has happened. This is something that a social script can be really helpful for.

EXAMPLE OF A SOCIAL SCRIPT TO EXPLAIN FOSTER CARE

My home is unsafe so I have to live in a different home.

This new home is called a foster home.

The adult in the foster home is called a foster carer.

The foster carer will take care of me and keep me safe.

There might be other children in the foster home.

In my foster home I might have things from my old home.

I will have my own bed in the foster home. This bed might feel different from my old bed.

I may have to wear clothes that feel, look and smell different from my old clothes.

I may eat foods that taste different.

There might be new smells, sounds and textures in the foster home.

There might be new rules in the foster home.

The foster carer will take me to school in the morning.

The foster carer will collect me from school at the end of the day.

The foster carer will take me to my foster home.

The Social Worker will decide when I see my mum and dad.

The court will decide if, or when, I can return to my mum and dad.

We hope you can see that when it comes to any placement or home move, Principle 1, 'Know your child (and his autism)', lies at the centre of everything. Use the strategies and core principles from Chapter 3 to help guide what's going to work well for your child.

How to support your child with contact

We're now going to look at 'contact', which is the name used to describe the time that children spend with their birth families, friends and other important people. It's also used to describe the ways in which information is exchanged between children and their family. There are many ways in which children stay in contact with important people including:

- face-to-face time
- telephone calls
- letter writing – commonly called 'post-box contact'
- exchanging DVDs and photographs
- emails and texts.

We don't really like the word 'contact' as a way of describing the time your child spends with important people. Contact is not a great word to use with a child who has autism, especially if he understands 'contact' in a literal way. The Oxford University Dictionary defines 'contact' as meaning 'the state of physical touching' and 'the action of communicating or meeting'. We think it's better to be more straightforward and explicit in what you call contact, by, for example, calling it 'the time you spend with your mum' (depending upon who the child is going to be seeing) or 'the letter we write to your birth mum'. In most non-fostering families, we wouldn't usually say, 'Let's go and have contact with your grandma'; instead we'd just say, 'Let's go and spend time with grandma.'

The decisions about what type of and how much contact your child needs are usually made by Social Workers, often as a part of the family court process. You may have had a lot, or only a little, input or influence over the contact arrangements and plans. Contact plans may be constantly under review and subject to change, as with a child in foster care. We can't tell you what amount or type of contact is right for a child with autism because each child has his own unique situation and needs. You need to do what works for him.

We know from our many conversations with foster and adoptive parents that contact can be very complicated, and it tends to raise a lot of mixed and powerful feelings for everyone involved.

Let's consider how we can make contact a bit more 'autism-friendly'. Remember that when we're thinking 'autism-friendly', we're encouraging you to consider our seven principles and remember the strategies from Chapter 3.

Here are some useful things to think about.

- What kind of environment works best for your child? This is Principle 7, 'Think environment'. If your child is spending time with his family in a particular venue, check that it works well for him.

- Are there any sensory issues that need thinking about?

- How can contact be made predictable for your child?

- How does your child do social communication and social interaction? This is Principle 1, 'Know your child (and his autism)'.

- How does he show any anxiety?

- How is your child understanding the situation? Are the rules and social expectations explicit and understood? Is there a social script for this situation?

Ideas for helping your child with contact that happens in a venue

First, think about the journey your child takes to get to contact. Consider:

- travelling using the same route to and from contact

- insisting on the same person taking your child to contact if you are not able to do it

- insisting on the same person (or people) supervising the contact – if it's supervised. We're well aware that it can be common for there to be different people supervising contact, but when your child has autism it is crucial that as many things about contact are kept the same. Having the same contact supervisors will help your child to cope better, and it means that this person will get to know your child and what works to help him feel comfortable

- sharing what you know about your child (and his autism) with the person who supervises contact – you can use our checklist in the Appendix to do this

- sharing what you know about your child with the person that your child is having contact with – if this is appropriate. It's always good to check what's useful to share with the birth family by talking with your child's Social Worker (if he has one). The main reason for sharing information is so that you and your child's family member can both use the same strategies to help your child feel 'just right'.

Think about the venue itself and, in discussion with Social Workers, consider:

- what will make the contact venue feel 'just right' for your child. For example, if the venue is too busy, can you ask for a quieter venue? If your child arrives at a contact venue that has a lot of people coming and going through the entrance, can it be changed so that he arrives at a different time or uses a different entrance?

- whether your child needs to visit the *same* room and place. Having contact in different places (that are not familiar) can add more sensory overload and possibly anxiety for some children. We're aware that social services can have difficulties with contact rooms, but this really is something that's very important. Ensuring that the same person supervises contact means that they can become aware of what might need to be changed in a contact room. For example, we've both observed contact happening for a child with autism in a room that's crammed with too many toys or is really small. This can make your child really anxious. Rooms that have space for your child to move around and that are not too busy with stuff can often work better

- whether your child is going to have contact at a new, unfamiliar venue. If so, think about whether it'll be useful for him to visit it *before* contact. This can give him the opportunity to familiarise himself with the sensory aspects of the place (this can also work well when your child visits any new place, such as the doctors)

- providing your child with a bag that contains consistent toys for contact, especially toys that help your child to manage anxiety. This bag can even be kept just for contact purposes.

These ideas all involved Principle 6, 'Be predictable'.

With your child, it can be helpful to:

- have a routine that is consistent both before and after contact. For example, after returning home from contact, your child could always have the same drink while sitting in the same place or spend time doing the same activity. Resist the temptation to add in unplanned activities or trips following contact. For example, if you collect your child from contact, then resist popping into the shops on the way home, unless your child has been prepared for this and is able to cope

- find out what your child understands about contact. You could use a visual timetable or a social script to explain it. We have given you an example of how to do this in picture form in Figure 5.3 and also as a written version.

AN EXAMPLE OF A SOCIAL SCRIPT TO EXPLAIN CONTACT

My name is Jamil and I am in Year 3.

I see my mum every month at a special building in town.

When I meet with my mum, other grown ups call this CONTACT.

Contact is where I get to spend time with my mum.

Mum sometimes brings things for me but not always.

When I see Mum at the contact, another person called Jane stays in the room. Jane checks that everything is okay.

We might have a drink and a snack at contact and play with toys.

When it is the end of contact I have to say goodbye to Mum and I can give her a hug if I want to.

After contact I go back to my house with my foster carer.

I see my mum every month. This is called having contact

We meet at a building in town.

We normally meet in the same room with the same toys

But sometimes the room is different

Mum sometimes brings things for me

But sometimes she comes without anything for me

There might be a screen on the wall that looks like a mirror with people behind it to watch us

We have a drink and a snack and play with toys.

At the end of the time me and mum say goodbye.

Then I go home with my foster carer.

Figure 5.3: An example of a visual timetable

Also use Principle 3, 'Understand the communication in your child's behaviour', to:

- be aware of the ways in which your child may show anxiety in relation to contact. Some children may show an increase in their rigid and inflexible interests, behaviour or routines before, during or after contact. An example of how this *could* be addressed is shown for our made-up girl Emily in the box.

Emily has lived in a few different homes. During the time she has been in foster care, and while she lived with her aunt, Emily has continued to see her birth mother for face-to-face contact. Emily's foster parent, Mary, noticed that Emily showed an increase in her need to keep her possessions in a certain way at around the time when Emily saw her birth mother. Mary spoke with Emily about contact and discovered that, although she enjoyed seeing her mother, she worried that she might return to live with her mother at any point without any warning. Mary decided to use a social script to explain to Emily that she would remain living with her. Mary used a visual timetable to show Emily what would happen in contact with her mother and that Emily would always return home with Mary.

Our seven principles and strategies from Chapter 3 can be used for any type of contact, whether it's through letter, email or phone calls. The key is to check what your child understands about contact and how it is labelled and explained and consider how you can make it a more predictable part of his life.

How to support your child with involvement from social care professionals

Let's think about how to help your child understand and cope with the ongoing involvement of Social Workers and other professionals. Professionals may be frequent visitors to your house or your child's school, particularly if your child is fostered. For example, fostered children usually have regular visits by a Social Worker and may be asked to give their views to placement review meetings. If you're a foster carer then your own agency Social Worker will regularly visit you. This ongoing involvement of Social Workers, although necessary, can add anxiety, irritation and intrusion to your child's life, regardless of whether he has autism or not. With autism in the mix, this ongoing professional involvement can raise some additional questions such as the following.

- How does your child understand the involvement of professionals and their visits? It can be difficult to know what meaning your child may be making from these visits. For example, it's possible that a home visit could lead to your child thinking that he is about to move home again.

- What is the Social Worker's understanding of your child's autism?

- How does your child communicate and interact with professionals?

- What impact does the visit have on your child's need for his routine to be predictable and 'the same'?

- What sensory experiences does the Social Worker's visit bring to your child?

- What are the aspects of professional involvement that could make your child feel anxious?

Good visits and meetings begin with the professional knowing about your child's autism.

Share what you know about your child with professionals

Always try to share what you know about your child and his autism with professionals. This uses Principle 1, 'Know your child (and his autism)'.

You will know just how important it is for your child to have his life in a predictable routine, with everything having a logical order to it – depending upon your own child's specific need for routine. So, when you know a Social Worker, or any other professional, is going to visit your child, make sure that they know some key information about your child. We're aware that there can be frequent changes in who your child's Social Worker is. This makes it even more important that you can quickly share what's relevant to a new Social Worker *before* they visit your child.

You could use the Appendix to share information. Often it is not enough for people, including professionals, just to know that your child has autism because it is different for each child. It can be common for people, including professionals, to hold false assumptions about what a child with autism is going to be like. You can use the Appendix to make sure that a Social Worker knows about any particular aspects of your child. For example, remember our made-up girl Emily and her need for her Lego® collection to be organised in a particular way (Chapter 3) – a Social Worker can avoid touching her Lego® during a home visit. Also, being aware of how a child communicates and interacts means a Social Worker can be prepared to adapt to this.

Make social work visits as predictable as possible

Ask your Social Worker to plan the time of their visit in advance and to arrive on time, especially if your child finds it difficult to wait. This uses Principle 6, 'Be predictable'. It can also help for the Social Worker to leave at a set time –

ideally a time that gives your child the opportunity to get back into his regular routine before bedtime (if the visit is in the evening).

If the Social Worker visits your child in school, predictability is also helpful. Ask the Social Worker to provide the time and day of the visit in advance, so that your child and his school know about it and can prepare. It's also helpful for your child's school to give feedback about whether the visit fits well into your child's school routine. There might be aspects of your child's routine in school that he would find difficult if disrupted – for example, visits during lunch-breaks or a favourite lesson.

Ask the Social Worker to organise their visit so that it happens during the calmest part of the day. It's best to avoid having visits on days when your child has been very busy or has had many transitions. This is Principle 5, 'Keep things calm'.

Consider using a visual timetable so that your child can see when the Social Worker will arrive and when they will leave. If it's needed, include a picture that shows that your child will not leave with the Social Worker so your child knows that he will stay at home.

If your child is made anxious by the Social Worker's visits, have a favourite activity ready for him to do during and after the visit. Tell the Social Worker what works well to help your child feel less anxious.

Consider using a social script to explain the visit. We've put an example of one in the box below.

EXAMPLE OF A SOCIAL SCRIPT FOR A VISIT BY A SOCIAL WORKER

The Social Worker's job is to make sure I am safe, growing and happy.

The Social Worker will come and see me in my foster home.

She may ask me questions about my foster home.

She may want to look in my bedroom.

She will talk to my foster carer.

After the visit, the Social Worker will leave the house.

I will stay in my foster home.

Overall, we hope you can see that, when it comes to visits by professionals, the key thing is to share what you know about your child (and his autism) (Principle 1) so that the professional can adapt their style to him. Keeping visits calm and predictable tends to work better for your child.

SUMMING UP

- Moving home is a massive change for your child.

- Good preparation for a change in placement begins with knowing about your child and his autism.

- Make an autism-friendly plan for the move.

- Collect and share as much information that you can about your child and his autism.

- Use what you know about your child to prepare him, yourself and your home.

- Children stay in touch with important people in different ways.

- It may be better to be more straightforward and explicit in how you label contact.

- Use what you know about your child and his autism to make contact fit his needs and help him feel 'just right'.

- Good visits and meetings begin with the professional knowing about your child and his autism.

Chapter 6

Attachment and Belonging

Let's move on to explore the topic of 'attachment', which is something that you've probably heard about. You were probably given some information about attachment while going through the fostering or adoption process. When it comes to autism, we've heard many foster and adoptive parents ask questions such as, 'What does attachment mean when my child has autism?' and 'Will parenting strategies that help to improve attachments in other children also help my child who has autism?' These are great questions to ask. We're going to explore what's known about attachment in children who don't have autism and then we'll think about attachment in relation to children with autism. We'll end with thinking about how you can develop an attachment with your child, which will help him to develop a sense of belonging with you.

What is an attachment and why do we need to know about it?

Attachment is the word that describes the bond or tie between a child and his attachment figure, usually his parent or main caregiver. At its most basic level, attachment is about a parent ensuring that her baby survives and a baby ensuring that he survives.

In the world of fostering and adoption, professionals and parents are encouraged to understand children and behaviour by using ideas from attachment theory. These ideas are incredibly useful for helping us to understand how fostered and adopted children are functioning on an emotional level.

When your child has autism, however, this will have a significant effect on the presentation of his attachment. It was thought at one time that a child with autism presented in the same manner as a child with attachment difficulties and that a child with autism is not able to have a secure attachment. These conclusions are wrong. Such misconceptions came around because the signs of attachment in a child with autism are subtler and harder to recognise than those in a child without autism.

All children can make attachments – children with autism are no different.

To understand attachment in a child with autism, you first have to realise that his style of relating, interacting and behaving is influenced first and primarily by his autism and then by his attachment. We're aware that this is getting complicated, so let's start with a basic understanding of what attachment is and why it is such a vital topic to understand. This will help us then to think about how autism can influence or interfere with the attachment process.

In a child with autism, you might see his autism rather than what his attachment looks like.

The easiest way to explore attachment is to look at how a child grows from birth onwards. The physical development process and the development of attachment are inseparable and intertwined, so we need to look at them both together. So, let's explore the attachment process in a typically developing child (i.e. one who doesn't have autism) and what usually happens between him and his parent during the first part of his life. We're going to be talking about a male child and his mother, although the process would be the same if we were talking about a female or male child and a male or female parent.

> Physical development and the development of attachment are inseparable and intertwined.

When a baby is born, he is completely dependent upon his mother for every single one of his needs. He needs his parent to keep him safe and protected and to meet his basic needs for food, shelter, warmth and so on. A baby is completely helpless, but thankfully he is born with some instinctive ways of letting his parent know when he needs something. He can cry! When he cries, he is letting his mum know that he needs her. When she picks him up and gives him what he needs, he is soothed. This sequence is repeated again and again during the baby's first few weeks and months, and it is this repetition of his most basic needs being met that helps him to learn that he is in a safe environment, where someone is going to meet his needs and keep him safe. Over time, this develops into an emotional connection between him and the person who is meeting his needs repetitively. Trust grows between the baby and parent. The child has developed the most basic form of secure attachment to his mother and, along with it, a significant but intangible sense that the world is a safe, secure place.

So, at its most basic level, attachment is about a baby signalling distress to his parent due to discomfort and his parent responding in a positive way by giving him what he needs and helping him to feel – not only a lack of discomfort (one force), but also comfort (a second force). There are therefore two directional forces that are both engaged in the nurturing of the attachment. We show this in Figure 6.1.

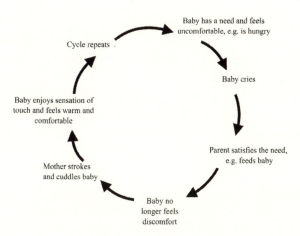

Figure 6.1: How attachment works

This sequence of a baby crying, or in some way letting his parent know that he needs something, and his parent then responding is played out again and again throughout a baby's early days and months of life. If this parent continues to meet her baby's needs consistently, then, through this repetition, the child will go on to develop what's called a secure attachment.

> Secure attachment develops when the baby's needs are met consistently over and over again.

There are lots of other things that are also going on during this attachment process as the baby grows and changes. A newborn baby uses his senses – touch, sound, sight, smell and taste – to attach to his parent. Babies need lots of physical contact such as cuddles, strokes and being held and gently rocked. This physical contact is a positive force for helping a baby to attach to his parent. It's been found that babies who are deprived of physical touch don't grow or develop very well.

> Physical contact and the baby's developing senses are a positive force for helping a baby to attach to his parent.

A newborn baby can already recognise the sound and smell of his mother from the time he has spent in the womb. He is born primed and ready to be interested in people's faces and eyes. A newborn baby is able to focus well enough to see his mother's face when he is held close to her. By the age of four weeks, a baby will prefer to look at a human face rather than something else. This interest in faces becomes more selective and, by the age of about three months, most babies show a preference for looking at their mother's face over any other faces.

As well as having a parent meeting her baby's basic needs, there are a couple of other processes happening that strengthen the attachment bond. These have the complicated sounding names of *interactional synchrony* and *reciprocity*, and they influence how a baby develops in his motor, speech and social abilities.

We've shown the things that influence the attachment process in Figure 6.2.

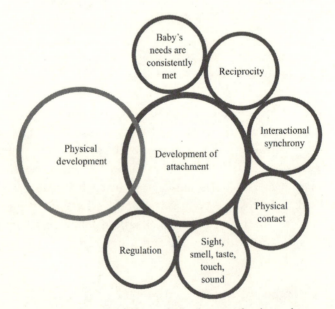

Figure 6.2: Things that influence the development of early attachment

What is interactional synchrony?

This is the name given to the baby's mirroring of his parent as he grows and becomes able to control his body. As a newborn, a baby does not have any control over his body, although he is able to focus well enough to see his mother's face and eyes. A baby looks at his parent and, as he develops more body control, he becomes able to mirror, or copy, what his parent does. Babies then gradually become able to begin to copy their parent's facial expressions, body movements and vocal sounds. When watching closely, it is noticeable that this copying falls into a rhythm. The baby and his parent become connected by being focused upon each other, mirroring each other and sharing this rhythm.

If you were to watch a mum with her baby, you would see this synchrony in action. For example, you might see a mum smiling at her baby and her baby smiling back. Her baby is showing a social smile, which usually develops at around six to eight weeks of age; before that age the chances are that the smile was due to wind!

You might also see a mum sticking her tongue out and her baby copying and mirroring this by sticking his tongue out too. This is interactional synchrony and it feels delightful to both mum and baby. It's like a conversation using actions.

Interactional synchrony also develops with the noises made by a parent and her baby. Parents tend to use a kind of sing-song and goo-goo voice with their baby. When a baby is about two months of age, he develops the ability to coo and gurgle back to his mum.

Overall, a baby and nurturing parent have lots of eye and face-to-face contact as they fall into this rhythm of using their body movements and speech sounds in response to each other, like a mirror. The degree of these body movements and speech sounds depends upon a child's development. For example, a baby who has just been born doesn't yet have any control over his body. A baby develops body and motor control over time. A baby develops control of his body in a sequence that begins with his head, moves down his body and moves from the centre of his body outwards. So, typically, a baby gains control over his eyes, head and neck before he develops more control of his shoulders, arms, hands and body and then his legs and feet. He learns to sit upright before he learns to walk.

Speech also develops in a sequence. A newborn baby will mainly communicate by crying but when he is about eight weeks old, he will begin to make cooing and gurgling noises. He then learns to babble before moving on to use single words.

> Interactional synchrony is what we call a baby's mirroring of his parent as he grows and becomes able to control his body.

These developments in a baby's growth are interwoven with the attachment process. For example, as a baby becomes able to control his body, this impacts upon how he interacts with his parent and how his parent responds. A baby learns to control his head, so he can turn and look for his parent. He learns to be able to move his eyes to follow his parent, and other objects, as they move.

What is reciprocity?

Alongside mirroring and synchrony, something called reciprocity happens. Reciprocity refers to the 'to and fro' that happens between a baby and his parent. If we look closely at the cooing and gurgling that goes on between a baby and his parent, we'll see that it's like a conversation that has a beginning, a middle and an end. The conversation is begun by either the baby or the parent, for example, when a parent says hello to him or says his name and he responds. They then 'chat' for a bit in a 'back-and-forth' manner until either the baby or parent ends the conversation. For example, a baby may turn his head away to signal that he needs a rest. The interaction follows a predictable sequence, a bit like a dance.

> Reciprocity is the 'to and fro' that happens between a baby and his parent.

This dance of reciprocity does not happen in isolation from everything else going on. It happens continuously, whilst all of the regular caring tasks are being carried out, such as feeding and nappy changes. It happens when the baby is distressed, for example, when a baby has wind and his parent winds him, or when a parent picks up and gently rocks her crying baby, who then stops crying and settles. This simple sequence begins with a child's distress and ends with the parent settling her baby. When this sequence is repeated again and again, the parent gets the message that 'holding and rocking' works when her baby is crying. The baby gets the message that this person, who he has learnt to recognise, can soothe him.

It is through this repetitive dance that a mother learns what her baby needs, how he signals it and how to help him feel settled and 'just right'. In attachment theory, this is called 'attunement'. It occurs when a parent is aware of, and can respond to, what it is that her child needs. Attunement is the ultimate kind of reciprocity.

> Attunement is when a parent learns what her baby needs, how he signals this and how to help him feel settled and 'just right'.

Reciprocity is also about the enjoyment that a baby and parent share together. They are 'being with' each other and this feels good to both the baby and the parent, i.e. it is mutually reinforcing. Babies respond to parents and parents also respond to babies. They are each actively involved in being with each other. This two-way relationship makes their attachment stronger.

> Reciprocity is about shared enjoyment.

What is regulation?

Throughout this dance of reciprocity and blossoming attachment, a baby becomes regulated and organised. When a baby is first born, he is a mass of sensory sensations and impulses. His brain, nervous system and body aren't very well organised and he has no control over his sensations or his body. You can see this in the jerky and random movements that he shows. He doesn't have a regular pattern for eating and sleeping and his main way of communicating is by crying. So, when a baby feels uncomfortable because he is hungry, he cries and it's up to his parent to hear the cry and to feed him.

By having his parent take care of all of his needs for feeds, nappy changes and everything else, a baby's body and brain learn to become organised. For example, during the first weeks of life, most babies fall into a regular routine of wanting feeds at certain times and of being asleep and awake at certain times. Through this routine, his brain is becoming regulated and organised. A baby can't do this by himself. He needs a parent to notice when and what he needs and to provide it in a timely way. The parent inevitably falls into a corresponding organised routine. In this routine, there is predictability, and it is this that adds to the baby's feelings of safety and security, reinforcing his knowledge that the world is a safe place.

> Regulation is what happens when a baby's brain and body organise together through predictable caregiving. Regulation promotes feelings of safety.

What about cognitive development?

During the first year of life, as the child and his mother develop a relationship in which they initiate interactions and responses to each other, he is also developing cognitive abilities. These include things such as being able to learn, play and remember things. Evidence of his growing memory means that he becomes able to anticipate what's going to happen next. You might have seen a three-month-old who, when placed on the nappy-changing table, holds his legs up, ready for a nappy change. A child also develops the ability to keep in mind a memory of his parent. We call this 'object permanence'. It is when a child knows that something exists, even during moments when it can't be seen. This means that the child has now learnt that when his parent leaves the room without him, she still exists.

A child's developing cognitive skills can be seen in his play. At first, babies are really interested in looking at objects, especially things with strong colours like black and yellow. As they develop, he starts to be able to touch toys with his hands. He may bat at the toys hanging from his mobile above his cot before then learning how to grab and hold them. Toys often end up in the child's mouth as he uses all of his senses to explore objects.

Over time, this play develops, so that at about two years of age, a child is able to do pretend play, such as when he pushes along a car while making the noises for it or using a spoon to feed a toy doll. As these skills develop more, he becomes able to use objects to represent things, such as pushing a wooden block (that is not a car) along and acting 'as if' it is a car. He starts to role play – perhaps becoming his favourite superhero.

As a parent plays with her child, all of this cognitive and play development stuff helps with their attachment and the relationship they have. The child learns how to play with his parent and how to take turns.

What is joint attention?

A child also learns something called joint attention. Joint attention is happening when two people, such as a child and his parent, are both focusing on the same thing. We can see an example of it when a child starts to point to show his parent something, for example, when a toddler points at an aeroplane in the sky to show his parent. There are lots of ways to get joint attention with someone. We can use our eyes to look at something so that someone else looks at it too, or we can point and show something.

Developing a sense of oneself and others

The next stage is that the child learns that he and his parent are two separate individuals. The child develops a sense of himself as someone separate who can do and feel things. He starts to use words such as 'me', 'mine' and 'you'. He develops the concept that his parent is different to him and that she will have her own actions, feelings and experiences.

Figure 6.3: Mother and baby in reciprocity

What does a secure attachment look like?

A secure attachment develops when a child gets his needs met by his parent in a way that is consistent and prompt most of the time. Signs of a secure attachment begin to be able to be seen at different stages during the first year of a baby's life.

If you were to observe a newborn baby, at first it would be hard to see signs of a clear attachment between him and his main parent. Very young babies appear to be fine when they are held or have their nappy changed by different family members – although laboratory studies have found that a baby prefers the smell of his mother and prefers looking at her face over someone else. In general, though, no obvious signs of distress can be observed in very young babies when they are with people other than their main caregiver, so long as their needs are being met.

> A secure attachment develops when a child gets his needs met by his parent in a way that is consistent and prompt most of the time.

Over the first few months of life, a baby learns to distinguish between his parents, his known family members and strangers. Most children show anxiety and become wary and fearful around strangers, from the age of about eight months to a year. This is also around the same time that children are generally learning to walk. This wariness can often be seen by him moving towards his parent (seeking proximity) when he feels unsafe. By doing this, the child is using his parent for safety. An example of this would be when someone new and unknown visits the house and the toddler moves closer to his parent, perhaps even hiding behind his parent's legs.

The growing toddler uses his ability to move around to explore and play. While exploring, he uses his parent as a secure base from which to explore his world. He will look back at his parent to 'check in' with her and will seek attention from her. If he were to fall and hurt himself, he would quickly go to or call out to his parent for help. His parent has, in his mind, become a secure base and reliable figure for safety and for comfort.

How do Psychologists examine attachment?

These changes in what a growing child can do has meant that we can watch attachment in action. An American Psychologist called Mary Main developed a measure for examining the attachment of a child aged between nine and eighteen months. She called this the Strange Situation. It involves having a child playing in a room containing toys and watching what he does when his parent enters and leaves the room and how he reacts when a stranger enters and leaves the room.

This measure has found that a securely attached child will use his parent as a secure base while he plays and explores the toys. When the stranger enters the room, the child will initially be a little wary but will interact with the stranger while his parent is present. The child then becomes wary of the stranger again when he is left alone with them. A secure child shows distress when his mother leaves him but is happy when she returns.

> Psychologists have developed ways of measuring the attachment of young children.

So, we can get some idea of whether even fairly young children have a secure attachment by watching what they do when they are playing and exploring and how they use their parents as a safe base. As children grow older and develop better memory and cognitive abilities, a secure attachment can be examined by using different methods.

By the age of four, children have a memory of their parent and are able to use dolls to represent people. This has led researchers to design procedures called Story Stems to examine attachment. These involve a child being guided to use dolls to represent himself and his parent. He would then be told the beginning of a story that involves his doll character being in distress, such as, 'Jamil has a poorly tummy.' He's then invited to finish the story using the dolls. A secure child tends to finish the story by showing his doll getting physically closer to his parent doll, who then does something to make him feel better again.

This Story Stem procedure works because by now the child has developed a sense of himself and his parent as being different people. He has a memory and has learned what to expect from his parent, and he is able to engage in representational play.

The child has developed what Bowlby (often referred to as the father of attachment theory) called an 'inner working model' of his parent, himself and his world. In a child with a secure attachment, this tends to look like this:

- Parent: 'My parent knows what I need,' 'My parent will give me what I need,' 'My parent will keep me safe.'

- Self: 'I am lovable,' 'I am important.'

- World: 'The world is predictable,' 'The world is safe.'

Figure 6.4 shows this internal working model.

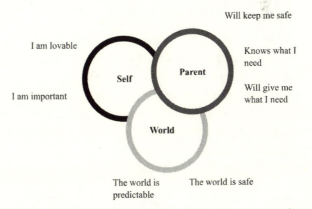

Figure 6.4: Internal working model for a child with a secure attachment

What other kinds of attachment are there?

As well as a secure attachment, research has identified two kinds of insecure attachment styles. Insecurity develops when a child experiences his parent as having not recognised or met some or all of his needs in a reasonable time.

There are two insecure attachment styles, which we've shown in Figure 6.5, alongside the secure style.

SECURE	INSECURE – AVOIDANT	INSECURE – AMBIVALENT
The parent meets their child's needs in a way that is consistent and prompt most of the time.	The parent mostly ignores or rejects their child. Child's needs have been ignored, dismissed or played down.	The parent has been inconsistent and unpredictable in recognising or meeting the child's needs. The parent may sometimes be quick to respond to the child but at other times may be slow or not respond at all.

Figure 6.5: Secure and insecure attachment styles

There are many reasons why an insecure attachment style may develop. These include reasons to do with the:

- parent, such as disability, depression, illness or problems with drugs and alcohol, which have interfered with the parent's ability, or availability, to provide the care that their child has required

- parent's attachment style – adults have their own attachment style, which they themselves developed during their childhood. An adult's attachment style tends to influence how they react to their child and how they meet their own child's attachment needs. A securely attached parent is far more likely to have a securely attached child

- child, such as illness or disability – these can mean that a child may not be signalling their needs clearly to their parent

- social circumstances, such as when a parent is stressed, preoccupied, overwhelmed or struggling due to challenges such as living in poverty, unemployment or a stressful environment. It is possible for this to affect their ability to focus fully and respond quickly to their child's needs.

Whilst a secure attachment is often considered to be the best style, this does not necessarily mean that an insecurely attached child will not go on to do well later in life. Attachment styles, whether secure or insecure, are really just ways in which a child has adapted to get his needs met in his current environment, such as in the following examples.

- A secure child's strategy is to seek out his parent for assistance.

- An insecure-avoidant child learns to ignore his needs or to meet them by himself. An avoidant child often learns to avoid seeking help from his parent.

- An insecure-ambivalent child learns to get his needs met by his parent by being loud, demanding or clingy. He can become preoccupied with getting his parent's attention by whatever means possible, such as crying loudly, throwing tantrums, being very clingy and demanding or exhibiting behaviour that he knows will draw his parent's attention. This child may even reject his parent or show a lot of anger when his parent does attend to him.

> Attachment styles, whether secure or insecure, are really just ways in which a child has adapted to get his needs met in his current environment.

A fourth category of attachment has been identified, which is called a disorganised attachment. This is not a 'style' in the way secure and insecure styles are. A disorganised attachment is different, because this is when a child has not developed any consistent strategy for getting his needs met or for making himself feel better. A disorganised child tends to show that he has a need by displaying behaviour that can seem strange, random and confusing.

For example, it could involve him seeking attention from his parent but then suddenly freezing or showing anger or aggression. It could involve him seeming to 'zone out' when he has a need. He just does not know what to do or whom to approach when he has a need or an uncomfortable feeling. He behaves this way because he has never had the experience of a parent taking care of his needs and regulating him.

Professionals often use the term 'attachment difficulties' to describe children. This term usually means that a child is having difficulties using his parent as a secure base for safety and comfort.

What are attachment disorders?

In addition to using attachment styles to describe attachments, professionals can also describe a child's difficulties in terms of attachment disorders. Many of the behaviours described for children with attachment disorders can appear to be very similar to those shown by children with autism – to such an extent that even some professionals can have difficulties spotting the differences.

Attachment disorders arise when something has gone extremely wrong in the child's early care

An example of this has been seen in children who spent their early months living in Romanian orphanages. These children spent long periods of time alone in their cots, because there were very few carers available and a great many children. Many of these children went on to behave and interact with people exactly 'as if' they had autism, when actually they didn't.

There are two kinds of attachment disorders listed in ICD-10 (that's the classification system we mentioned in Chapter 2). They're called:

- Reactive Attachment Disorder of Childhood (RAD)

- Disinhibited Attachment Disorder of Childhood (DAD).

What is Reactive Attachment Disorder (RAD)?

Children who have RAD show emotional disturbances such as difficulties with empathy, aggression towards people when they are distressed (or when someone else is), withdrawal from people or fearful hypervigilance.

They usually struggle in lots of different situations and respond to others in ways that are contradictory or ambivalent. These children behave and react as if they don't know how to be with people or how to respond to them. RAD usually develops when a child has experienced very neglectful early care, so it's not surprising that these children have not learned how to be calm and settled when they are in situations that involve others.

Children with RAD usually show differences in their emotional responsiveness to others. This can include them being unable to show any emotion in situations that would usually evoke emotion. For example, if a child snatched a toy from another child, the child who lost the toy would usually protest in some way, probably by crying or trying to grab the toy back. A child with RAD may respond differently. He may instead stare at the child who took his toy and not do anything. The child with RAD may simply pick up another toy and carry on playing as if nothing untoward has just happened. Children with RAD can show a limited range of emotion and emotions that don't seem to fit the situation that they're in. They may become angry, sad or scared for no obvious reason.

Overall, children with RAD find it really difficult to develop relationships and attachments with others. They do not seem to need, or seek out, comfort or support from their parents. Their experiences have sadly taught them that people cannot be relied upon or trusted to meet their needs and keep them safe and soothed.

What is Disinhibited Attachment Disorder (DAD)?

Children with DAD have also experienced poor early care. These children seek out a lot of attention from people, regardless of whether they are familiar people or strangers. These children may behave as if they know strangers and will willingly wander off with them.

It would not be unusual for a child with DAD to have gone on a supermarket trip with his foster carer and to have wandered off and been found in the restaurant, sitting on the lap of a bewildered stranger. These children can behave in very over-familiar ways with strangers, such as chatting and hugging them. They seek a lot of physical and verbal affection and contact. This is, of course, extremely risky behaviour for the child and tends to be very confusing for the adults around them.

We've shown these two attachment disorders in Figure 6.6, which shows how children with RAD and DAD are different.

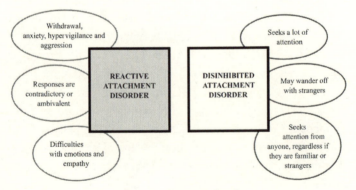

Figure 6.6: Attachment disorders

A QUICK SUMMING UP

- Attachment is all about survival and safety.

- Attachment requires two people: you need to have a child and a parent in interaction together to form an attachment. It is not possible for a child to form an attachment by himself.

- Attachment involves synchrony, reciprocity and regulation.

- Attachment and child development are inter-connected.

What is different about attachment in children with autism?

Attachment becomes more complicated to unpick when a child has autism. This is because autism impacts upon both the processes involved in developing an attachment and how a child displays his attachment. These 'different'-looking displays of attachment can easily be misunderstood by those who do not understand the subtleties of autism.

When children move into foster care at an older age, and where it is known that they experienced neglect and trauma, it can be common for them to show some difficulties with social communication and social interaction; these difficulties can appear very similar to those shown by autistic children. This means that if an assessment of the child is needed to advise on whether autism is part of the picture, it is so important that it is carried out by a professional knowledgeable in *both* attachment and autism.

Autism can affect the development of attachment because of differences in the following areas:

- sensory processing

- social communication and social interaction

- rigid or inflexible interests, behaviour and routines

- interactional synchrony, joint attention and reciprocity

- theory of mind.

Figure 6.7 is a reminder of our main aspects of autism.

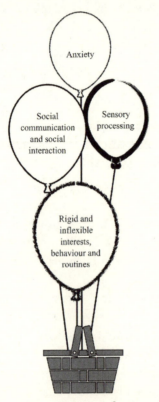

Figure 6.7: Aspects of autism

The best way for us to explore how autism can affect the different areas that are involved in making, and showing, an attachment is for us to look at them in turn using examples. While we do this, remember that autism is diverse, and each child is unique. This means that any one child may show some, none or all of these differences.

Sensory processing

As we've already discussed in Chapter 1, a child with autism perceives his world in a different way to a child who doesn't have autism. Sensory information, such as touch, sights, sounds, smells and tastes, will be perceived and processed by him in his own unique way. He may have some sensory things he prefers and some that he finds overwhelming, over-stimulating or even painful. You'll remember that we've talked about this in terms of a child's window of tolerance, and this window can move and change.

A child may be distressed by sensory stuff that doesn't seem to bother other children who don't have autism. These challenges can first become an issue when a child is a baby and cannot communicate his discomfort. Sensory stuff may also be an issue for older children who find it hard to communicate their 'different' experience. In babies, for example, it may mean that blankets or clothes that should feel soft to most babies feel rough, irritating or even painful to a baby with autism. Or sounds that would be soothing to most babies may feel way too much for a baby with autism.

It may be really hard for a parent to know how to settle her baby when he's distressed if she doesn't know which sensory things are too much or are uncomfortable or painful for him. For example, it can be hard to work out that a baby can't cope with the usual kinds of baby blanket, clothes and nappies.

Many of the things we expect babies to get comfort from may be very uncomfortable for a baby who has autism and sensory differences.

A baby with autism can also be very sensitive to touch, finding it over-stimulating and even painful. A baby without autism will thrive on being held, cuddled and rocked. But what if a baby with autism finds this too much? Lots of parents of children who have autism report that their baby squirmed away from cuddles or their bodies became really rigid when they were cuddled. This lack of wanting or accepting physical affection is completely unthinkable to many parents. It can feel really hard and will often impact on their identity as a parent.

When a child has lots of sensory difficulties, he can be disturbed or upset more easily, and it can be really hard for his parent to get him into a routine that works well. This affects how the parent is able to settle and regulate her child. Lots of children with autism can have difficulties with regulation, for example, with being able to sleep.

Many birth parents of children who were later diagnosed with autism describe their child as having been a baby who was far harder to soothe and settle than other children. Or they say that their child had a particularly difficult or grouchy temperament. A non-verbal child with autism will often not use his voice to signal to his parent that he is distressed and needs something. This can leave his parent feeling unsure as to whether he has an unmet need or not. These experiences are really hard for parents who don't know that their child has autism and has been experiencing lots of sensory information in a different way that's causing them discomfort.

A child may also struggle to process sound. He may respond to sounds such as the vacuum cleaner but not turn and look when his name is called. Many parents report having first felt that something was wrong with their baby when he didn't show a response to them calling his name. In fact, many referrals for autism have begun with parents worrying that their child may be deaf.

Many children with autism struggle to process lots of different kinds of sensory information at the same time. For example, some can only process one type of sensory input or have a bias towards one sense over another. He may have strong visual processing but struggle with auditory information. This could mean that he can process the visual information coming from his parent's face and body language but struggles to process the noises and words that are being said. For this child, when his mother comes towards him whilst talking and using her face and body to communicate, he could find the amount of simultaneous sensory information too much and overwhelming. This may lead to him moving out of his window of tolerance and withdrawing or freezing as a way of shutting out all of this stuff.

Sensory processing affects the child's attachment because, naturally, most parents use touch, sight, sound and smell as the primary ways of relating to their child, accepting signs back from their child that their relationship is developing and seeing that a bond is forming.

Social communication and social interaction

Social communication and social interaction are involved in the attachment process. A child with autism can show behaviours that some parents can consider to be strange or that look similar to a child who has attachment issues. Some common examples of this are given below.

- A baby with autism may not cry to signal that he is feeling uncomfortable. Or he may cry a lot to signal that he is feeling discomfort caused by things that a parent cannot easily identify.

- A child with autism may not be so interested in looking at people. He may not watch or look out for his parent when exploring his world or his toys.

- A child with autism can be focused more on his own interests than interacting with his mother or others. This can make his interaction with his parent seem very one-sided.

- A child with autism may not seek comfort from his parent when he has hurt himself or has another need such as hunger.

One of the core things about a child with autism is that he is not naturally going to fall into the usual patterns of developing typical, clear, two-way interactions with his parent.

Rigid or inflexible interests, behaviour and routines

It is very common for children with autism to exhibit repetitive behaviours or to show a preoccupation, or obsession, with a particular interest. Obsessive play with certain toys or activities can make it difficult for a parent to play with her child. These children often need to follow a very rigid routine, typically find change, flexibility and spontaneity extremely difficult and can find it hard to tolerate anyone else trying to play with them. This can make it tricky for a parent to be playful and spontaneous. Play that involves surprise – such as peek-a-boo or hide and seek – can become stressful. It can also be stressful if a parent behaves in a different way to usual or suggests an activity outside of the normal routine.

Interactional synchrony, joint attention and reciprocity

A baby with autism may not be as interested in looking at eyes and faces. He may be less responsive to his parent, for example, not smiling in response when his mother smiles at him. And he may be less likely to initiate interaction with his parent. This means that there might not be much eye-to-eye and face-to-face contact between a baby and his parent. This impacts upon that interactional synchrony process of the child mirroring movements, facial expressions and sounds that we examined earlier. If a baby is not looking at his parent, he will not begin to learn to copy movements and faces.

Likewise, autism can affect how speech develops, so if a child is non-verbal or doesn't coo, gurgle or babble like children normally would, he is not going to make or mirror vocal noises or begin to learn to chat with his parent.

The reasons that children with autism have such difficulty getting 'into sync' with their parent are not fully understood from a clinical perspective, but it is clear that it can affect the attachment process.

As play develops, when playing with toys the child may be unable, or far less likely than other children, to point at things or to show them to his parent so that they can direct their attention to the same thing. They don't develop joint attention.

Children with autism also often can't do the 'back and forth' of reciprocity, or they do it in a different way. This can be seen in the difference or lack of any of the usual social responses, such as smiles, facial expressions and vocal noises. Many birth parents of children who were later diagnosed with autism have described how their child could not 'reciprocate'.

As a parent, this can feel really difficult because reciprocity feels very important to us as human beings. Noticing a response makes us feel that the other person is listening, watching and paying attention to us. It makes us feel that they care about what we do, feel and say. It is about connection and enjoyment. When a child can't do this, the parent is often left feeling as if something very significant is missing in her connection with her child. It can be very hard sometimes to develop moments of chatting and playing with a child with autism.

Theory of mind

We touched upon theory of mind in Chapter 1. Children with autism can struggle with this, which can make their interactions with parents (and others) very one-sided. A child can find it hard to understand that another person has her own emotional and mental experience or that the experience they have may not be the same as the child's.

The child may therefore approach his parent when he needs something but not try to create interactions or moments of them being together.

Difficulties in this area can make it hard for a child to read facial expressions. He may be able to recognise a facial expression, such as what a happy or sad face looks like, but be unable to link that knowledge to knowing what the person may be feeling inside. When a child can't understand or process this, he's unlikely to respond to people in an expected way.

We know that we've covered a lot of complex ideas, so we've tried to simplify them in Figure 6.8.

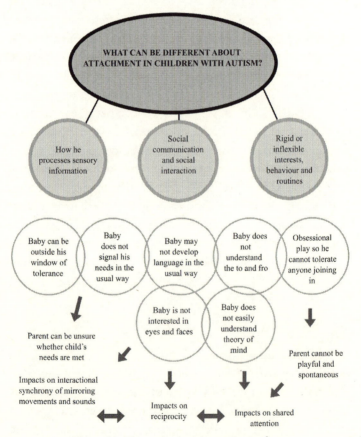

Figure 6.8: How autism may impact on attachment

What's known about attachment in children with autism?

Nearly everything that we know about attachment is based upon research looking at children who do not have autism. There has been very little research focused upon exploring what attachment looks like in children with autism. From what is available, we know that:

- children with autism *can* and *do* form secure attachments to their parents

- attachments may look different in children with autism

- it can be more difficult to work out how secure a child's attachment is, especially when his autism is more severe or if he has other developmental difficulties such as a learning disability.

Most of the research on attachment in autism has been carried out on children who are being raised by their birth parents in the usual circumstances, i.e. not fostered or adopted children.

Most of what we know about attachment is based on children who don't have autism.

Using the Strange Situation procedure that we mentioned earlier, it's been found that just over half of children with autism develop a secure attachment to their birth parent. This figure is about the same as for children without autism who develop secure attachments (65%).

Using this same procedure, it's been found that children with autism show a preference for their parents over strangers, and they will still use their parent as a secure base. What is interesting, though, is that the way in which a child with autism uses his parent as a secure base 'looks different' to the way in which a child without autism does this. For example, an autistic child may physically touch his parent less, or he may not use his eyes to communicate his distress to his parent.

How do you know whether a child has autism or attachment difficulties?

We hope you now have:

- a good understanding of what attachment styles and attachment disorders are

- the knowledge that autism can affect both the development of attachment and how it looks.

With this in mind, we're going to briefly touch upon why confusion frequently arises between attachment and autism.

Attachment issues are very common in adoption and fostering circles. Attachment has become a bit of a buzzword that's commonly jumped to as the first explanation for a child's behaviour. By understanding attachment, we can be better equipped to notice and explore a child's behaviour and think about what it might mean.

Both children with attachment disorders and children with autism show differences from other children in how they approach and respond to their parents and to others. However, these different behaviours have arisen for very separate reasons. An attachment disorder arises when a child has experienced poor and neglectful early care. Autism, on the other hand, is not caused by poor parenting or by neglectful early care; children are born with autism.

We've talked about attachment styles and attachment disorders so that you can be aware of what they are. Knowing about attachment can help you to notice what behaviours your autistic child may show and why some people may wrongly assume that his difficulties are due to attachment problems rather than being about autism. Of course, your child is more likely to have experienced poor care earlier in his life, and he will have experienced disruptions in his attachment relationships. However, when your child has autism, the autism-bit will have much more influence over his behaviour and relationships than attachment per se.

We don't want to encourage you to 'diagnose' whether your child has autism or attachment difficulties. We instead want you to be informed so you can think about what is going on for your child.

To help analyse the many differences and similarities in how children with autism or attachment difficulties interact, think and behave, a Clinical Psychologist called Heather Moran and her colleagues developed a framework called the Coventry Grid.

This framework highlights that there can be a difference in how interactions *feel* when an adult interacts and has a relationship with a child who has attachment difficulties compared with a child with autism. For example, a parent's relationship with a child who has attachment difficulties tends to have a strong *emotional* feel to it. This can be played out by some children with attachment difficulties seeming able to start a relationship but it then becoming emotionally intense and stressful. A child may want to play with his parent in one moment but then reject her when he has a need such as hunger. A parent can *feel* as though her child's behaviours are kind of 'personal' to her – as though her buttons are being pushed for a response.

In contrast, a parent's relationship with a child who has autism tends to have more of a *matter-of-fact* and logical feel to it. There is often less emotion within it. This parent does not feel that her child is trying to push her buttons.

Professionals have also observed that the trigger for a child's distress can differ depending upon whether a child has autism or attachment difficulties. When a child has attachment difficulties, it tends to be his interactions with others, especially his parents, that trigger distressing feelings and difficult behaviours. Whereas when a child has autism, it tends to be something about his environment, such as an unexpected change or a sensory input like a loud noise, that triggers distress and difficult behaviours.

Overall, however, because the presentation of children with autism can be so varied, even professionals can find it challenging to say for definite whether a fostered or adopted child has difficulties with attachment or with autism. It is, of course, possible for a child to have difficulties in both areas.

Your child's experience of parents

When your child is fostered or adopted, it is fairly likely that he has had earlier experiences of parents who did not give him good care or were neglectful or abusive towards him. This makes it likely that he will have some attachment issues in addition to his autism.

Whatever your child's past experiences, your task is to give him a different and positive experience of parenting – one where you can get to know him, understand him and meet his needs (our Principle 1). This may be a completely novel experience for him, and it may take him bags of time to get used to it.

How to influence attachment when your child has autism

To understand your child's behaviour and relationships, remember that he will be influenced first and most by autism, and then by his attachment experiences.

> When your child has autism, the autism is the 'lens' for how he perceives, understands and interacts with everything and everyone in his world, including you.

The good news is that developing security with an autistic child is not really that different from developing it with a child who does not have autism. Through spending time with your child, and viewing him through a lens of autism, you can start to work out what his specific likes, dislikes and needs are, and how you can respond to him. It is through this that your child will grow to understand that you 'get where he is at' and your attachment bond will form.

What really stands out from all the attachment stuff is that a child who develops a secure attachment (whether he has autism or not) has a parent who is:

- predictable and consistent

- sensitive to her child's needs, in tune and timely – knowing just what he needs when he needs it

- able to help him feel physically and emotionally safe

- able to take joy in her child and enjoy spending time with him

- able to be with her child, providing the time and space to explore and enjoy activities together.

We hope you will see some similarities with our overriding principles from Chapter 3. All children respond better when things are *calm*, when things are *predictable* and when you can *get alongside him* and *understand the communication in his behaviour*.

Some ideas for developing your child's attachment with you

Use Principle 1, 'Know your child (and his autism)', to work out what helps him to be 'just right'.

If you know what helps him feel 'just right' and how he can be helped to stay within his window of tolerance, then, over time and with a lot of patience and repetition, he will learn that you know him and that you can help make things better for him.

Use Principle 2, 'Get alongside your child', to find ways to connect and be with him. Remember that you can find a connection with him by being together, being alongside him and being parallel to him. You don't need to be constantly involved in talking to him and playing *with* him. Lots of us can find it comforting to be with someone just sitting side by side, enjoying a quiet space together. It can be the same for your child. So, don't be discouraged if he doesn't respond to you or if he doesn't try to actively include you in his experience. It can be just as valuable to share his world with him.

When you are with your child, include a mix of activities that are about 'to and fro', and have times when you just focus on being *with* him and *sharing* his experience of his favourite objects and sensory things. In Chapter 3 we spoke about ways you can join him in his play by being alongside him. For example, if he enjoys looking closely at objects, such as looking at parts of things (like spinning the wheels of a toy car or watching the washing machine when it's on the spin cycle), you could sit next to him and do the same. If he likes to line toys up, you could do it with him. By doing this, you will be giving him the message that, 'I can be with you.' You're letting him know that he's important.

Use Principle 1, 'Know your child (and his autism)', and think about his sensory world. If your child shows a fascination with colours, you could join him when he explores this. For example, you could get hold of lots of sunglasses with different coloured lenses or sheer, coloured scarves to look through with him.

If he has a fascination with touching certain textures, you could get hold of fabrics with different textures and explore them with him through touch.

If you notice that your child responds to your voice, you could spend time singing and talking to him to connect with him.

Think carefully about touch. If your child can't process touch, and perhaps is hypersensitive, connect by using touch in a more low-key way. For example, you could both touch objects that he likes in a way that means you also touch each other – such as pressing your fingers into putty or drawing around each other's hands. The important thing is to be led by your child's sensory processing, so if he finds squidgy textures unpleasant, you might need to use something different. Or you could look at an object together while sitting close to each other, so you're touching side by side.

Think about how your child understands social communication. For example, if your child struggles to process facial expressions, he may connect more with you by focusing on your voice. You could make silly noises together or you could read and sing to him. You could connect through an object he likes – for our made-up child, Jamil, this might be his toy cars. You could draw or paint together and explore craft materials. Again, be guided by any sensory sensitivities your child has.

If your child cannot understand speech, engage him in activities that don't rely on talking. Try playing games that are non-verbal, such as rough-and-tumble type play. Obviously only do what's safe, and avoid games that trigger any sensory difficulties.

Just as you wouldn't insist on a deaf child listening to you, don't insist on your child talking to you when he doesn't understand. Spend time with him in the non-verbal world. Think about how you can adapt to be with your child. Some of us find it easy to be on our own in solitude while some of us like to be surrounded by people. Find a way to be in solitude alongside your child – even if it means that you get your quota of social and people contact at another time.

Use Principle 6, 'Be predictable': being predictable, reliable and consistent in your parenting behaviour and responses to him will help him to develop security in you. Put in place a regular daily routine and think carefully about all those everyday transitions. Use appropriate behavioural boundaries that fit with what his behaviour is communicating. These will help him to feel safe.

SUMMING UP

- Attachment is all about survival and safety.

- Attachment requires two people. You need to have a child and a parent in interaction together to form an attachment. It is not possible for a child to form an attachment by himself.

- Attachment involves synchrony, reciprocity and regulation.

- Attachment and child development are interconnected.

- Autism can affect the development of attachment in many ways.

- The most important thing is for your child to experience you as:

  - predictable and consistent

  - sensitive to his needs, in tune and timely

  - someone who can help him feel physically and emotionally safe

  - someone who can find joy in him and enjoy being with him.

Chapter 7

Life Story, Loss and Trauma

In this chapter, we're going to explore how to help your child:

- understand her life story and the reason for being fostered or adopted

- recover from trauma and loss.

While doing this, we're going to keep our seven principles from Chapter 3 in mind.

Before we explore these topics, we want to acknowledge that there are many reasons why children come into foster care. Your child may have experienced harm, such as neglect or abuse, or she may have been at risk of harm when living in her birth family. Or your child may not have experienced any abuse or neglect. She may have moved into foster care for a period of respite.

We think it's important to say that in families where the adults are already struggling with parenting, an autistic child can be at a greater risk of being harmed or neglected by her parent compared with a child who doesn't have autism. There's no one explanation for this, although it's probably because some parents can find autistic children harder to parent. Parents may also have many competing demands on them that make parenting a child who has extra needs more difficult. In Chapter 6 we explored attachment and what can sometimes go astray in that process – all of these things can make parenting extremely challenging.

Some children with autism may enter the care system during a crisis, such as when a family has been unable to cope with a child's difficult behaviour. As we've explored earlier, difficult behaviour can be related to the child's environment, such as sensory overload that has made a child distressed and overwhelmed. For many different reasons, some parents can find this too difficult to cope with and can react in abusive ways. It can be a complicated situation for parents, and we certainly wouldn't want to judge any parent, especially as most do set out wanting the best for their child.

How to help your child understand her past and the reason for being fostered or adopted

We're going to organise this section by encouraging you to think about this topic in the same way that you can approach tricky behaviours or difficult transitions. Remember our assessment–formulation–intervention model from earlier chapters. You can use this to help you explore what might work best for your child when it comes to life-story stuff. So, using *what*, *why* and *how*, let's consider the following questions.

- *What* is life-story work?

- *Why* does a child need to know about her past and life story?

- *How* should life-story work be done?

What is life-story work?

Life-story work is a broad term that's used to describe ways in which a child is given information about her life and what has happened to her. Life-story work could be done through a series of structured sessions with a professional, or it could be something that you, as her parent, do in a more ad-hoc way when you talk to her about her past life.

Why does a child need to know about her past and life story?

Most people agree that it's important for all of us to know where we come from and what has happened in our lives. It's no different for children with autism. Life-story work helps children to have clear knowledge about what has happened. It helps a child to develop her identity. It helps give a sense of safety by, for example, explaining the reasons for previous home moves – this can give reassurance that there won't be any further moves because those reasons no longer exist (if that's the case).

How should life-story work be done?

Social care departments can differ a lot in terms of how and when (or even if) a child has life-story work. Some departments will provide a series of sessions on life-story work, for example, when a child is being adopted. Other departments may provide a life-story book – we say more about this later. From experience, we know that very often it is foster and adoptive parents who do the bulk of the talking about the past with their child.

There are no set rules about when or how any child, with or without autism, should have life-story work. Every child's needs are different, so use what you know about your child and her autism – Principle 1 – to guide it.

For example, let's think about our made-up child, Jamil, who is moving from fostering to adoption. We know that Jamil struggles to understand situations and he likes to know what is going to happen, and when. So, it's better for him to be given information about his life, and the reasons for his previous moves, *before* he moves to adoption.

Jamil's autism may also mean that he needs extra time to process information about his life and he needs repeated opportunities to do this. So, having this information *before* he moves to adoption means that he'll have more chance to take in what has happened to him and why. It will also allow adults to check how much he has understood. Giving Jamil the information in a book also makes it easier for adults to be as sure as they can be that Jamil's understanding of what has happened is the same as theirs (and that the same words are used to describe things). It also gives Jamil the best chance of revisiting the information about his life.

So, decisions need to be made about *when* to do life-story work. It's also important to think about *how* to do life-story work. Again, a focus on Principle 1, 'Know your child (and his autism)', is crucial.

When considering *how* to do life-story work, it's important to understand how your child's autism may affect her understanding about her past and the reasons why she is fostered or adopted. Here are some examples of how autism may affect understanding.

- Your child may not understand concepts such as 'fostered', 'adopted' and the 'past'. Social scripts can be really helpful for explaining what things and people mean. The key thing is to use the same labels and language for describing things. In Chapter 5 we looked at a social script to explain a 'forever mummy'.

- Your child may have a poor concept of time, so referring to the 'past' or 'where you used to live' could be confusing. Some children can find it helpful for their life to be shown visually in a timeline that starts with birth and finishes with 'today'. It could show pictures of your child at different ages alongside a picture (or a name if you can't get a picture) of who she lived with and things she did (such as 'holiday with grandma') or favourite activities. The key is to keep it simple and have clear labels on the pictures.

- Your child may have a focus only on the 'here and now'. It can be common for an autistic child to focus only on her current life and not upon her past. Some children might be very black and white about it and say, 'I live here now,' so the past is no longer important to them. This doesn't mean that you should assume that life-story work is not important. Instead, create a book and regularly remind your child that it exists.

- Your child may have rigid (black-and-white) think-ing. Your child may see herself, her autism or any difficult behaviours she has shown as the reason for her being in foster care. She may label herself as being 'bad'. It can help to have the reasons for her being fostered or adopted clearly written out like a social script or shown in a picture. Black-and-white thinking might also influence your child to expect you to act in exactly the same way as a previous parent. Social scripts can help to explain why parents can be different from each other.

- Your child's differences with social communication and social interaction may make it difficult for you to know how she feels about her life. For example, she might not show any emotion, or she may show an inappropriate emotion such as laughing, when you talk about the past. She may ask lots of irrelevant questions or ask nothing at all. Remember that Principle 1, 'Know your child (and his autism)', should mean that you understand that how your child looks on the outside is not necessarily a reflection of how she is feeling on the inside.

- Your child's rigid and inflexible interests, behaviour and routines may be important. For example, she may focus only on her daily routine. Rather than her wondering about the reasons *why* she is in care, she may instead be more concerned about how foster care might interrupt her daily routines. She may be anxious about what is going to change in her life and what will stay the same. Creating a predictable environment for your child (Principle 6) will help her to understand that things do not necessarily have to change.

• Your child may ask repetitive questions, and this does not necessarily mean that she doesn't understand the answers. This repetition could be part of her autism. If she keeps asking the same question, just keep on giving the same answer because it will be what she needs to feel safe.

Of course, as with all things autism-related, every child will be different. But, by being aware that autism can affect your child's understanding, you can explore *how* to give her the information she needs.

> When thinking about life-story work, think about how your child's autism might affect her understanding and how she communicates about her past.

An example using our made-up girl, Emily

Let's think about our made-up girl, Emily, to explore *how* to help her to know her past.

Emily has lived in a few different places and she currently lives with Mary. We know that Emily struggles with her social communication and social interaction. She has a rigid and inflexible interest in Lego® figures – she likes to organise them in a set way and she can't play imaginatively with them. We know that Emily struggles with understanding other people's points of view and she has a need for sameness and predictability.

Bearing this in mind, Mary and Emily's Social Worker decide the following.

- Emily needs the same person to talk to her about her life story. They decide that Mary is the best person to do this because she knows how Emily shows that she is anxious, and she knows how to help Emily feel 'just right' again.

- Emily needs to be given information about her life during a series of sessions that happen at the same time, and in the same place. This makes it organised and predictable (Principle 6) rather than this topic being brought up and sprung upon Emily when she is not expecting it.

- Emily needs to be given factual information about what has happened in her life.

- Emily needs to be given simple explanations about why she moved into foster care. Mary decides to use straightforward sentences such as, 'Your mum took a lot of drugs and alcohol. The drugs and alcohol stopped your mum from being able to do tasks, such as getting you ready for school.' These simple explanations are a good starting point for Emily to ask questions when she is ready to, rather than bombarding her with a lot of information. Even though Emily is now 12, she needs simple explanations.

- Emily will struggle to understand all of the reasons for why her mother neglected her. She will struggle to understand her birth mum's feelings and thoughts. Mary uses a social script to explain why Emily's mother could not look after her. We have put an example of this in the text box.

A SOCIAL SCRIPT TO EXPLAIN WHY SOME PARENTS CAN'T RAISE THEIR CHILDREN

A mum needs skills to be able to raise her child. There is a lot to know about caring for a child. A mum needs to be able to know how to keep her child safe, fed and clean. A mum needs to know when her child needs to sleep and when she needs to go to school. A mum needs to know how to teach her child how to get dressed and use the toilet. A mum needs to know when to say 'yes' and when to say 'no'.

Love is important for children. Sometimes a mum does not know how to show love to her child. Sometimes a mum can show love but cannot do the other things that her child needs, such as being fed, dressed, kept safe and taken to school.

Sometimes a mum does not have the skills she needs to raise her child. A mum may not have learned the skills. A mum may not be able to do the skills she has learned when she is drunk, on drugs or unwell.

A word about life-story books

Your child may have a life-story book. Adopted children should all have one. Fostered children may or may not. A life-story book is a bit like a scrapbook or photograph album. It's usually put together by a social care professional using information from records and by collecting photographs and other information from the birth family. It typically contains information about your child's birth and early life and explains what went wrong and how a decision was made for your child to be fostered or adopted.

Life-story books vary a lot in how much, and what kind of, information they include and how child-friendly they are. We've seen life-story books that range from helpful to unhelpful. Some have contained the basic details of a child's life, while others have contained too much. Some life-story books have portrayed the child's story in a way that seems a bit unreal, with the serious reasons for care having been glossed over. This can be unhelpful, as it does not fit the facts for the child.

We think that life-story books should always be made specifically for each child. No two books should be the same, because each child has her own story and her own way of understanding it. If your child has a life-story book that does not fit her needs, we encourage you to approach your child's Social Worker (if she has one) to get it changed or to change it yourself. Take copies of the pages and reorganise them into a way that works better. Here are some ideas that can work well.

- Begin with where the child lives now (with you) and work backwards in time.

- Keep it simple and stick to the facts.

- Keep the story logical and matter of fact.

- Try to avoid including pictures that have confusing facial expressions, especially if faces are something that your child struggles with.

- If you include difficult or traumatic past events, label the situation and the emotion, for example, 'Your mum and dad used to fight, and that could have frightened you.'

- Consider whether your child needs to have a set time to look at her life-story book – using Principle 6, 'Be predictable'.

- Look at the book with your child in a quiet place and when your child is in a receptive mood. Be aware of your mood and whether you are feeling calm – Principle 5, 'Keep things calm'.

- Don't be overly focused on trying to read the whole thing. Match where your child is at. She may want to look repetitively at certain pages – and that is okay.

Don't get stuck with the idea that the information always needs to be in a book form. Some children get more value from having a box that contains pictures and objects from their life. Objects can include things that smell – such as your child's birth mother's favourite perfume.

Other children get a better sense of their life by having frequent visits to places that they used to visit (if this is safe and appropriate). This could even be videoed for your child to watch again. You could audio record your child's life story so she can listen to it rather than her having to look at something. If it's appropriate, people from your child's birth family could even be asked to audio record stories from a book that your child has enjoyed or of something (appropriate) that happened to your child.

We hope you get a sense that when it comes to life-story work, the main thing is to use Principle 1, 'Know your child (and his autism)', to work out what's going to work best. Remember that the strategies from Chapter 3 are also helpful.

Helping your child recover from past trauma and loss

Trauma and loss can be a difficult subject to face, but the good news is that the ideas and strategies that we've covered already will help your child recover from difficult experiences.

Let's explore what we mean by trauma and then think about some ways to help your child.

What do we mean by trauma?

Children are said to have experienced trauma when they've witnessed or been directly involved in a traumatic event.

These events can be 'simple' or one-off events, such as being in a car accident or natural disaster. Most fostered and adopted children will, however, have experienced what's called 'complex' trauma – they've been exposed to trauma from difficult home lives that have involved issues such as domestic abuse or parental drug or alcohol use. The words 'complex trauma' and 'developmental trauma' both describe trauma that's happened in a child's relationship with her parents or other family members because of neglect and abuse (emotional, sexual and physical). Such experiences impact on a child's attachment and her physical and emotional development.

Some children may have Post Traumatic Stress Disorder (PTSD). PTSD symptoms include:

- reliving memories of the traumatic events, such as flashbacks or nightmares. These memories are distressing and can be triggered by something that reminds the child of the event, although there isn't always an obvious trigger

- feeling emotional, numb and being detached from people or surroundings

- avoiding or fearing places, people or things that remind the child of the traumatic event

- being easily distressed

- finding it hard to concentrate

- showing hypervigilance

- having tantrums

- showing problems with sleep, eating and toileting.

A child may not have a memory of the traumatic event, although her body may have a 'sensory' memory of it. This means that a situation may not feel right for a child, but she might not know why. Many children show that they've experienced trauma through their behaviour rather than by talking about it. Many children can find it difficult to use words to tell their story. A child may have developed behaviours that made her feel safe when she lived in a difficult place, but these behaviours have become a bit more of a problem once she has moved to a safer place. It's always useful to think about your child's behaviour and what it means, using the ideas from Chapter 3.

What's tricky is that many traumatised children can actually show symptoms that are similar to autism. This can make it difficult for you (and professionals too) to tease out how much she has been affected by trauma in her relationships and life. The good news is that by focusing mostly on helping her to feel 'just right' and safe, you are also helping her to recover from trauma.

Some extra things that a child with autism can find traumatic

We want to highlight that some everyday *simple* events can be felt as 'traumatic' by an autistic child, even when another child would not be disturbed at all. For example, if a child with autism is not helped to have her sensory needs met – by, for example, not being allowed to take sensory breaks during the school day or by being forced to stop doing her repetitive behaviours ('stimming') – this can feel traumatic. Also, if a child's social needs are not met – by, for example, 'forcing' her to be in a social group – this can feel awful for her. For example, if our made-up foster child, Emily, was forced to spend a lot of time with other girls her age (perhaps through an intention to make her learn social skills), she could feel a lot of distress and it may highlight to her how 'different' she is.

Unfortunately, a child with autism is more likely to be bullied by her peers, especially at school, and particularly if she looks or acts different. We want to encourage you to be watchful for this and to talk to your child's school the moment a problem becomes noticeable. Bullying is always best sorted out by being proactive and by not allowing it to grow.

Dealing with trauma and loss from the bottom up

It's tempting to dive straight in to sorting out a child's trauma, perhaps by talking about the difficult events and the losses she has had. However, this doesn't usually work very well until you have some other bits in place. Children recover best when we start from the bottom and think first about making their daily lives predictable, safe and calm. This means thinking about all of the ideas from Chapters 2 and 3, which focused on you getting to know what helps your child to feel 'just right' by using our seven principles.

In Figure 7.1, we have used a pyramid to show how the bottom stuff is the foundation upon which other interventions can rest.

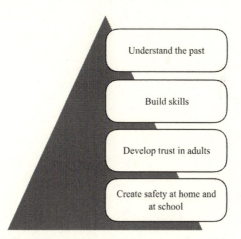

Figure 7.1: Pyramid for recovering from trauma and loss

Let's look briefly at this pyramid. We hope that you quickly realise that these are ideas that you'll be aware of from earlier chapters – you may already be using them.

Create safety at home and school

The main things are to:

- have routine and a structure to her day

- manage her environment

- be aware of her window of tolerance

- help her with transitions

- understand her behaviour and what she is communicating

- be calm and predictable.

In a nutshell, you begin with the 'here and now' and focus on all of the things that help her to feel 'just right' and safe. This feeling of safety will come and go for your child throughout the day. Remember that as your child moves through her day, she will experience transitions and changes that can move her from feeling 'just right' and safe to then feeling unsafe and overwhelmed. Your role is to help her manage this and to tell her school and other people what she needs when she is with them.

By being aware of her window of tolerance, you can help her to feel safe. When a child has experienced trauma, her window may be smaller, and it may change in different situations. For example, she might associate specific places, people and objects with traumatic events. Be a detective for her and try to notice if she shows fear and distress about certain things.

It's worth knowing that we usually convey safety to our children through social cues such as smiles, eye contact and laughter, and we use our bodies differently when we are feeling safe. It's important therefore to think about this from the point of view of your autistic child, who may process social communication and social interaction differently. Explore what you know about your child's autism (Principle 1) to work out how you can best convey safety to her. It can be tempting to tell your child that she is 'safe now' but words don't teach, particularly when your child struggles with language and communication. Your child will learn more from having repeated experience of feeling safe in your home.

By helping your child to develop ways to feel safer more of the time, you're giving her a good foundation for being able to understand her past difficult stuff. Children deal with the difficult, 'big' stuff more easily when they feel settled and safe.

Develop trust in adults

This connects to the bottom level of safety. From you being a parent who is calm, patient, predictable and someone who can understand her, she will over time develop trust in you. You will become her secure base.

If her school also works to help her cope within that environment, your child will learn that other adults can be trusted.

Build skills

This level is all about helping your child to develop everyday skills. As her parent, you will be wanting to help her develop and learn skills. These are skills that most children need to learn such as becoming independent with self-care (such as dressing herself and brushing her teeth) plus skills for living in a home (such as table manners) and a community (such as how to walk safely by a road). You might also need to add in specific skills such as learning about privacy by, for example, teaching her the 'underwear rule' – a way to teach children on the autism spectrum about sexual abuse that you can find on The National Autistic Society website.

Understand the past

When your child feels safe in your home, you can help her to understand her past using ideas that we looked at earlier in relation to her life story. Remember, though, that there is no such thing as a child having 'finished' or 'done' her life-story work. Life-story work, and understanding losses and events, is something that your child will need to return to at various points during her life. Whenever life story issues come up for your child, it's useful always to think *safety first* and work on making sure your child is feeling safe and 'just right' *before* looking at difficult aspects of her past.

> Recovery from trauma and loss begins with feeling safe.

When to seek help for your child

We encourage you to seek help as and when you need it. The proverb 'it takes a village to raise a child' is very true for fostered and adopted children, especially when autism is in the mix. There are some specific therapies that might help when your child has experienced trauma, including the following.

- Theraplay® involves a child and her parent. It aims to build attachments, relationships and experience of play and enjoyment together (Booth and Jernberg, 2009).

- Dyadic Developmental Psychotherapy involves a child and her parent. It's based on what is known about attachment, developmental trauma and brain development. It focuses on helping a child to learn to trust her parent (Hughes, 2017).

- Trauma-Focused Cognitive Behavioural Therapy can help older children learn to understand and cope with anxiety and trauma symptoms.

- Eye Movement Desensitisation and Reprocessing (EMDR) is a technique, usually used within another therapy. It uses bilateral stimulation of the body through side-to-side eye movement, tapping or sounds to help a child's brain to process traumatic memories.

When looking for a Therapist, we encourage you to find someone who is qualified to work with trauma and autism. All of these therapies would need careful assessment to check that they will fit your child's needs. If therapy is offered, it'll need to be adapted for your child.

Make sure that anyone who works with your child knows how her autism affects her. Remember the balloons from Chapter 1 and share what you know using the Appendix. Be her advocate!

SUMMING UP

- Children are fostered and adopted for many different reasons.

- Life-story work is the name given to the ways in which a child is given information about her life.

- Use what you know about your child and her autism to guide life-story work.

- Autism could affect your child's understanding about her past and the reasons why she is fostered or adopted.

- Traumatic events can be simple, one-off events or complex and involving many events. Many fostered and adopted children have experienced complex trauma.

- Recovering from trauma is a bottom-up process. It involves:
  - creating safety at home and school
  - developing trust in adults
  - building skills
  - understanding the past.

- Recovery from trauma and loss begins with feeling safe.

- Seek help as and when you need it.

- Specific therapies can help your child with trauma and loss.

Chapter 8

Looking After Yourself

Throughout this book, the focus has been on how you can think about your child, understand him and consider what he needs to feel 'just right'. All of this takes a lot of energy, patience and persistence, so we want to end by encouraging you to take the time to think about what *your* needs are and how you can make sure that *you* also feel 'just right'. So here are some things for you to consider.

Understand autism, so you don't take things personally

When your child has autism, he's not choosing to behave in certain ways and he's not choosing to find things difficult. He really is doing his best. If it feels like he's saving up all of his difficulties for when he gets home, this is just him showing you that he feels safe enough with you to express himself.

If you understand that he might be struggling with social communication and social interaction, has rigid and inflexible interests, behaviours and routines that he has to follow, finds processing a lot of everyday sensory information difficult and he gets anxious but can't necessarily tell you that, this will help you to understand what might lie behind some of his behaviour.

Understand autism so you can be realistic about what can change (set realistic goals)

If you understand what your child's strengths are as well as his difficulties, and know the signs of his teacup overflowing or him moving outside of his window of tolerance, you will know what he can manage. If you can also get alongside him and understand what lies behind his behaviour, you are in a great place to know what change is manageable. Be realistic and take it one step at a time.

Understand what helps you to feel 'just right'

We've spent a lot of time talking about getting to know your child and his autism, especially what helps him to feel 'just right'. We encourage you to do the same for yourself. Take a moment to think about what makes you feel stressed, how you show stress and what helps you to feel better. Consider spending some time exploring what your own sensory likes and dislikes are and what activities calm you.

Stock up your own reserves: you can't keep on giving without taking something good in!

This simply means making sure that you give yourself plenty of the things in your life that make you feel good.

Get your own social interaction needs met

Schedule social time for yourself. Sometimes, parents of an autistic child tell us that they can feel as if they are not important to their child – as if they are somehow 'disposable' because their child does not seem to respond to them. Children with autism often give less or different kinds of feedback to their parents. Remember that your child does have a relationship with you, even if it feels different to what you expected. It can be common for a parent to feel that they are missing out on a social or emotional connection with their child. If this resonates with you then make sure you get your own needs for a social and emotional connection met by regularly spending time with valued friends and family.

Build up your network of support: connect with other parents of children with autism

Link up with local autism groups such as those organised by The National Autistic Society and attend trainings.

Ask your fostering or adoption team if they have any meet-ups with other parents.

Ask at your local child development centre library about groups or events that are happening locally.

Find other people who can look after your child for a bit, so you can have a break

If you have supportive friends and family, ask them for support with childcare (if you're a foster parent then check this with your Social Worker).

Explore whether there is a local short breaks service available in your area.

Ask your fostering and adoption team about options for respite care and support with childcare.

Understand why it can be exhausting to care for your child

Be aware of the signs that you may be becoming exhausted and get what you need at the earliest opportunity. Don't be put off asking for help.

Develop your resilience to any difficult behaviours that your child may show

We hope that what we have covered in this book will help you to be the best parent you can be to your child, but you will need to take a step back at times and look at the bigger picture. There will be times when it is hard (remember to ask for help) and there will be times when you feel as if you are doing a bad job. But if you understand your child and his autism, and follow our principles, we hope that this will help you to ride out some of the trickier times.

Chapter 9

Seeking Help and Resources

Places to find help and support

We've included things here that are easy to find and that we think are helpful.

Websites

The National Autistic Society: www.autism.org.uk

For information on Theraplay®, visit: www.theraplay.org

For information on Lego®-Based Therapy, visit: www.bricks-for-autism.co.uk

For information on Dyadic Developmental Psychotherapy (DDP), visit: https://ddpnetwork.org/uk

For information on EMDR, visit: http://emdrassociation.org.uk

For lots of practical resources, especially for working with your child's school, visit: www.reachoutasc.com

Books

There are loads of books available that deal with autism. Here are our current top reads.

Books to help you understand autism

The Girl with the Curly Hair series of books is very good for a no-nonsense approach to helping everyone understand just why things are so difficult for people with autism. The books are written by Alis Rowe, an author with Asperger's syndrome, and they are some of the most accessible and informative books we have come across. Titles include:

- *Asperger's Syndrome in 5–8 Year Olds*

- *Asperger's Syndrome in 8–11 Year Olds*

- *Asperger's Syndrome in 13–16 Year Olds*

- *Asperger's Syndrome and Anxiety.*

Although they have Asperger's syndrome in the title, they really are fantastic for anyone with autism, and not just girls.

Freaks, Geeks and Asperger Syndrome: A User Guide to Adolescence by Luke Jackson, a young person who has autism, published by Jessica Kingsley Publishers.

Kids in the Syndrome Mix of ADHD, LD, Autism Spectrum, Tourette's, Anxiety, and More! by Martin Kutscher, published by Jessica Kingsley Publishers. This is a book for parents that is good at helping to navigate the issues around co-occurring difficulties.

Been There. Done That. Try This! An Aspie's Guide to Life on Earth, edited by Tony Attwood, Craig Evans and Anita Lesko, published by Jessica Kingsley Publishers.

For specific issues relating to girls with autism, read *Asperger's and Girls* by Tony Attwood and Temple Grandin, published by Future Horizons. *The Girl with the Curly Hair* series is also good for thinking about some of the particular difficulties girls might have.

Books that have ideas about how to play and interact with your child

Play-Based Interventions for Autism Spectrum Disorder and Other Developmental Disabilities by Robert Grant, published by Routledge.

Books for understanding autism in schools

Working with Asperger Syndrome in the Classroom: An Insider's Guide by Gill Ansell and *The Essential Manual for Asperger Syndrome (ASD) in the Classroom: What Every Teacher Needs to Know* by Kathy Hoopmann, both published by Jessica Kingsley Publishers.

Books to help work together with your child's school and about school transitions

How to Support Pupils with Autism Spectrum Condition in Primary School and *How to Support Students with Autism Spectrum Condition in Secondary School*, both by Lynn McCann and published by LDA. These are great for practical resources.

Books that help understand anxiety

From Anxiety to Meltdown by Deborah Lipsky, who has autism herself, published by Jessica Kingsley Publishers.

Starving the Anxiety Gremlin: A Cognitive Behavioural Therapy Workbook on Anxiety Management for Young People by Kate Collins-Donnelly, published by Jessica Kingsley Publishers. There is an equivalent book for younger children, by the same author called *Starving the Anxiety Gremlin for Children Aged 5–9*.

Asperger's Syndrome and Anxiety from *The Girl with the Curly Hair* series gives a really valuable insight into why anxiety can be such a problem in autism.

Books that you can read with your child or that your child can read

The ASD Feel Better Book by Joel Shaul, published by Jessica Kingsley Publishers.

All About Me: A Step-by-Step Guide to Telling Children and Young People on the Autism Spectrum about Their Diagnosis by Andrew Miller, published by Jessica Kingsley Publishers.

Different Like Me: My Book of Autism Heroes by Jennifer Elder, published by Jessica Kingsley Publishers.

My Autism Book. A Child's Guide to THEIR Autism Diagnosis by Glòria Durà-Vilà and Tamar Levi, published by Jessica Kingsley Publishers.

General bibliography of books and papers

Booth, P. and Jernberg, A. (2009) *Theraplay: Helping Parents and Children Build Better Relationships through Attachment-Based Play* (3rd edition). San Francisco: Jossey-Bass.

Bowlby, J. (1969) *Attachment and Loss, Vol. 1: Attachment.* New York: Basic Books.

Dissanayake, C. and Crossley, S. A. (1997) 'Autistic children's responses to separation and reunion with their mothers.' *Journal of Autism and Developmental Disorders 27,* 295–312.

Gray, C. (2015) *The New Social Story Book.* Arlington: Future Horizons.

Hughes, D. (2017) *Building the Bonds of Attachment* (3rd edition). New York: Rowman and Littlefield.

Kenny, L., Hattersley, C., Molins, B., Buckley, C., Povey, C. and Pellicano, E. (2016) 'Which terms should be used to describe autism? Perspectives from the UK autism community.' *Autism 20,* 4, 442–462.

Main, M. (2000) 'The organized categories of infant, child, and adult attachment: Flexible vs. inflexible attention under attachment-related stress.' *Journal of the American Psychoanalytic Association 48*, 4, 1055–1096.

Moran, H. (2010) 'Clinical observations of the differences between children on the autism spectrum and those with attachment problems: The Coventry Grid.' *Good Autism Practice 11*, 2, 44–57.

Russell, G., Rodgers, L. R., Ukoemunne, O. C. and Ford, T. (2014) 'Prevalence of parents reported ASD and ADHD in the UK: Findings from the millennium cohort study.' *Journal of Autism and Developmental Disorders 44*, 31–40.

Siegal, D. J. (2013) *Parenting from the Inside Out.* New York: TarcherPerige.

Finding a professional

There are different ways to find a professional to help. This information is mainly about services in the UK, but if you are reading this book in another country then your health insurer or primary health care physician should be able to help you to find the right route to assessment. If your child is looked after, then your Social Worker should be able to help you.

If you are an adoptive parent, the first step should be to talk to your child's GP who will be able to tell you what NHS services are available locally, how they might be able to help and how to access them. It's also important to seek support through your local Social Services Post-Adoption Team so they can assess your support needs and help to signpost you to the best service.

If you are a foster carer, the first step should be to talk to your child's Social Worker who can then arrange a referral for a health assessment, which could be with a Paediatrician.

Some areas will have specialist services set up for the emotional and mental health of fostered children. These services should be able to assess what is going on for your child and what might help. They may be able to explore whether your child has autism or help refer your child to the right service.

For Occupational Therapy and Speech and Language Therapy, you can get a referral through the NHS via your GP, through social care funding or you may be able to fund some assessment and input yourself.

You might be able to get a referral to a Clinical Psychologist through your GP, but it may not be straightforward because most Clinical Psychologists work in CAMHS and getting referred to CAMHS is not easy.

We just want to mention that adopted children in England can access the Adoption Support Fund and this can be used to fund work on adoption issues, although it cannot be used just to fund work on autism. Luckily, many therapies that are approved for adoption issues also work well with autism. Some areas also have specific CAMHS teams for looked-after and adopted children; it varies across the country so we're not going to say too much about what these teams might look like because it might not be like that in your area.

If you decide to look for a private-sector Therapist, we hope the following resources will get you to where you need to be. You should make sure that the person you see is registered by the Health and Care Professions Council (HCPC); anyone you find through the following websites will be registered.

Independent sector professionals
Speech and Language Therapy
To find an independent sector Speech and Language Therapist, you can go to the Association of Speech and Language Therapists in Independent Practice: www.helpwithtalking.com

Occupational Therapy

To find an independent Occupational Therapist, you can search on the Royal College of Occupational Therapists website, which has a section on independent sector Therapists: www.rcotss-ip.org.uk

Clinical Psychology

To find an independent Clinical Psychologist, you can search on the website for the Association of Child Psychologists in Private Practice. Just be aware that this website lists both Clinical Psychologists and Educational Psychologists, but each person's entry will tell you what they are. www.achippp.org.uk

Getting to Know my Child

In this appendix, you'll find a checklist that covers the different areas that are involved in autism. We hope it helps you to think about what you already know about your child and what you might want to find out. You can use this to collect information from people who know your child. Your child may also want to contribute to it.

You can use this appendix yourself and you can also share it with other people who spend time with your child, such as family, friends, School Teachers and Social Workers.

You can download a copy of this checklist to print out at: www.jkp.com/catalogue/book/9781785924057

GETTING TO KNOW MY CHILD...

Social communication

This is how my child communicates...

- Verbal, speech:
- Use of words:
- Understanding of words:
- Non-verbal:
- Use of gestures:
- Facial expressions:
- Body language:

Adults can help my child communicate by…

The kinds of situations my child can find hard to understand are…

The kinds of social rules my child finds hard to understand are…

Anxiety and feeling 'just right'
When my child is happy

- he shows this by…
- he needs adults to…

When my child is upset

- he shows this by…
- he needs adults to…

When my child is tired

- he shows this by…
- he needs adults to…

When my child is angry

- he shows this by…
- he needs adults to…

When my child is sad

- he shows this by…
- he needs adults to…

When my child is distressed

- he shows this by…
- he needs adults to…

When my child is anxious

- he shows this by…
- he needs adults to…

When my child is overwhelmed

- he shows this by…
- he needs adults to…

The situations that make my child anxious are…

My child likes to escape to places that are…

Social interaction

- When with younger children, you'll see my child…
- When with same-aged children, you'll see my child…
- When with older children, you'll see my child…
- When with adults, you'll see my child…
- When with parents, you'll see my child…
- When with a mixed age group, you'll see my child…
- When something goes wrong, you'll see my child…
- When with strangers, my child will…

Rigid and inflexible interests, behaviour and routines

- My child's favourite things to do with his body are…
- My child's favourite objects are…
- My child's favourite activities are…
- My child can get stuck with doing…
- Adults can help my child move on from doing… by…
- Routines that are important to my child are…
- Things that my child has to do when in a new place are…

- Things that my child has to do when meeting new people are…
- The parts of daily life that my child needs to be the same are…

Everyday transitions

- My child manages everyday transitions by…
- My child copes better at wake-up time by…
- My child copes better at bedtime by…
- My child copes better when taken into school by…
- My child copes better with transitions during the school day by…
- Other transitions that can be tricky for my child are…
- Adults can help with these tricky transitions by…

Sensory needs

Visual stuff my child likes:	Visual stuff my child can't tolerate:
Smells my child likes:	Smells my child can't tolerate:

Sounds my child likes:	Sounds my child can't tolerate:
Body positions and sensations that my child likes:	Body positions and sensations that my child can't tolerate:
Kinds of physical touch my child likes:	Kinds of physical touch my child can't tolerate:
My child responds to physical touch by…	

My child's zone of physical space with other people is…

The things that help a place be 'just right' for my child are…

Subject Index

lunchtime 130, 141
mental health, autism and 49–50
mirroring 177–8, 196–7
multi-disciplinary team 70–2
neurodevelopmental difficulties
    (definition) 23
occupational therapy 234
over-familiar behaviour 28
'passport', student 136
PDA (Pathological Demand
    Avoidance) 59–60
physical touch 157
placement transitions 144–6
play
    difficulties with 27
    play dates 117
    role of 85–8
Post Traumatic Stress Disorder
    (PTSD) 217–8
predictability, importance of 97–8
prevalence of autism 56
Reactive Attachment Disorder (RAD)
    189–90
reciprocity 178–9, 196–7
regulation (child development) 180
relationship, development in 119–20
rigidity 36–9, 90, 196
routine 38–9, 90, 97–8, 196
safety, creating feeling of 220–1
school
    autism and 123–4
    break-time 129, 141
    environment 100–1
    going home 130–1
    lining up 141
    lunchtime 130, 141
    separation from carer in morning
        128–9
    student 'passport' 136
    transition between different
        schools 132–6
    transitions in the day 126–36
    see also teachers
secondary school 132–3
secure attachment 182–4
selective mutism 30

self-care 224–7
sensory diet 41, 107
sensory processing difficulties
    39–41, 193–5
sensory strategies 108–9
separation from carer in morning
    128–9
services, organisation of 49–50
sleep 118, 125–6
social communication difficulties
    and attachment 195–6
    body language 32–3
    empathy 34–5
    gestures 33
    overview of 27–9
    play 27
    spoken language 29–32
    tone of voice 32
social scripts
    contact 165–6
    forever mummy 152
    foster care 160–1
    overview of 104–5
    parenting 214
    social worker visit 170–1
Social Stories 103–5
social workers' input 145, 148–9,
    167–71
spectrum, autism as a 25–9
speech and language therapy 233
spoken language 29–32
Story Stems procedure 184–5
Strange Situation procedure 184,
    199
student 'passport' 136
support
    books 229–31
    finding a professional 232–4
    seeking help 120
    self care 224–7
    websites 228

teachers
    'assessment' by 68
    variety in skills of 123–4
terminology 18, 20–2, 58

Author Index